THE GOLDEN FLEECE AND THE HEROES WHO LIVED BEFORE ACHILLES

ILLUSTRATIONS BY WILLY POGANY

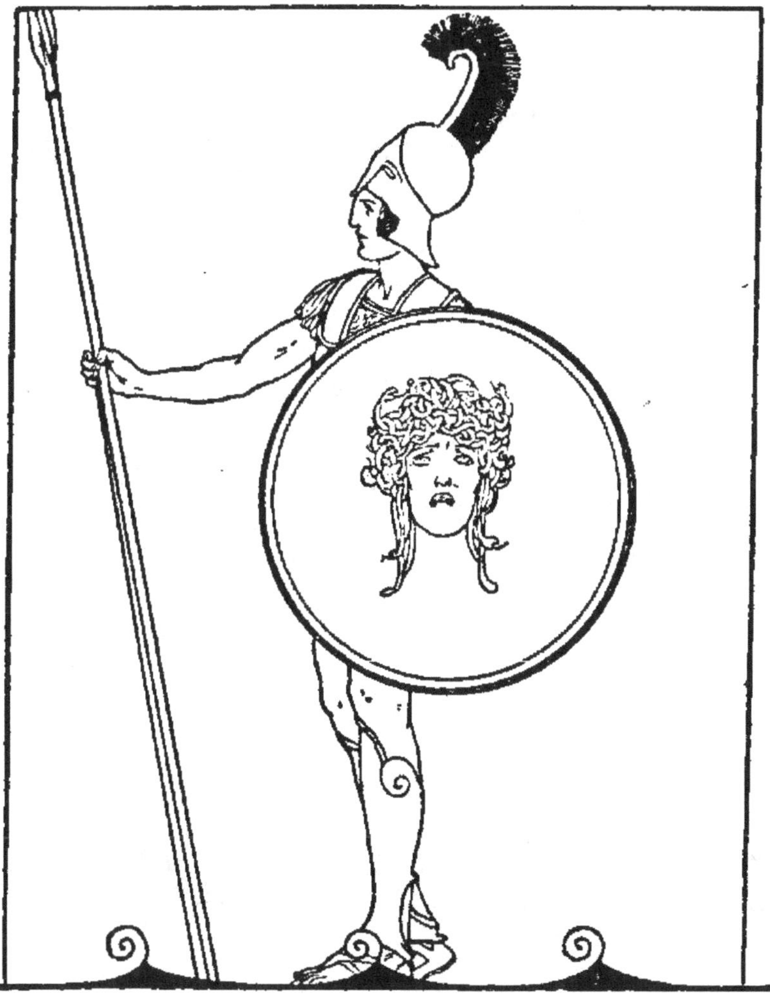

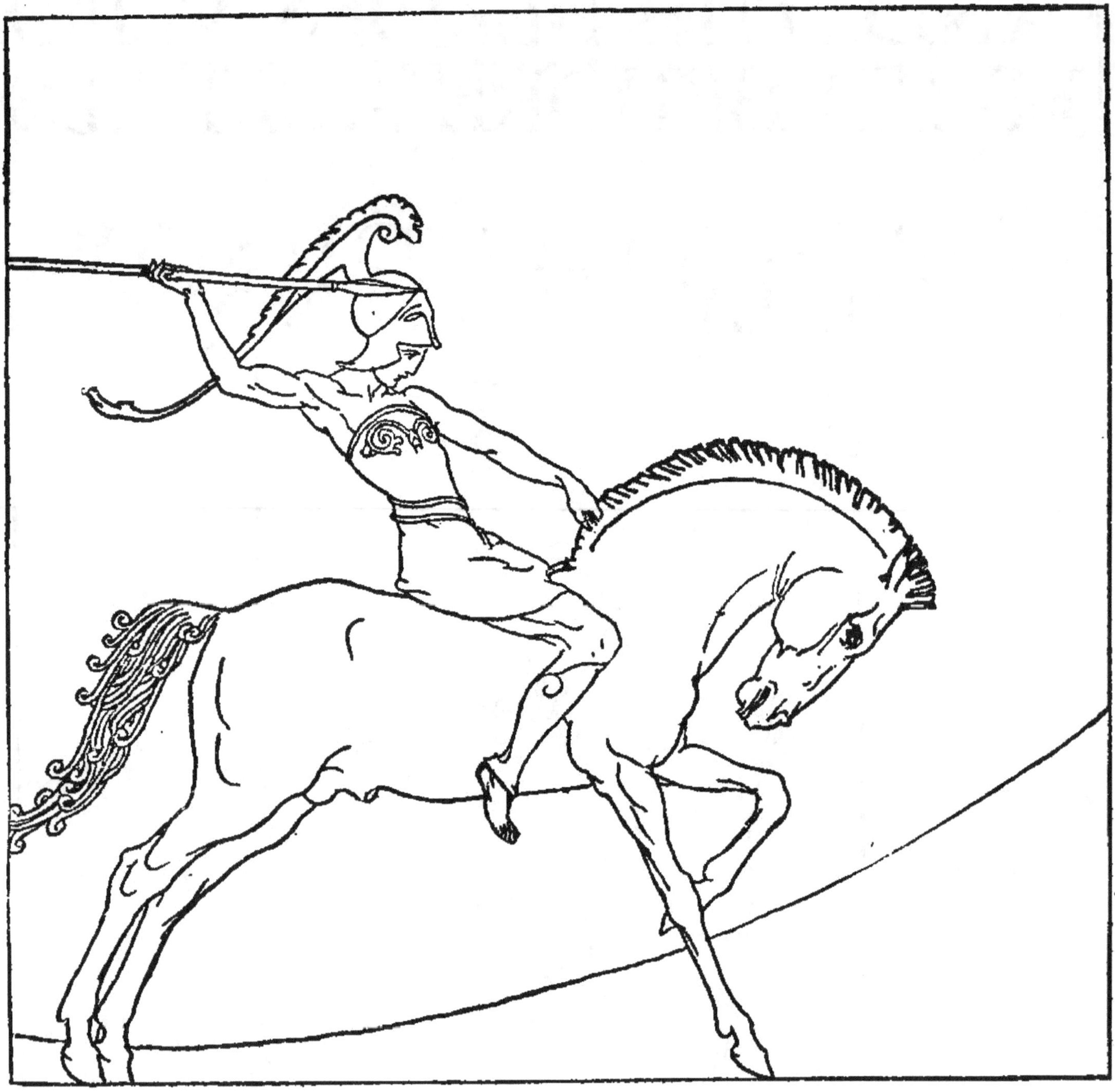

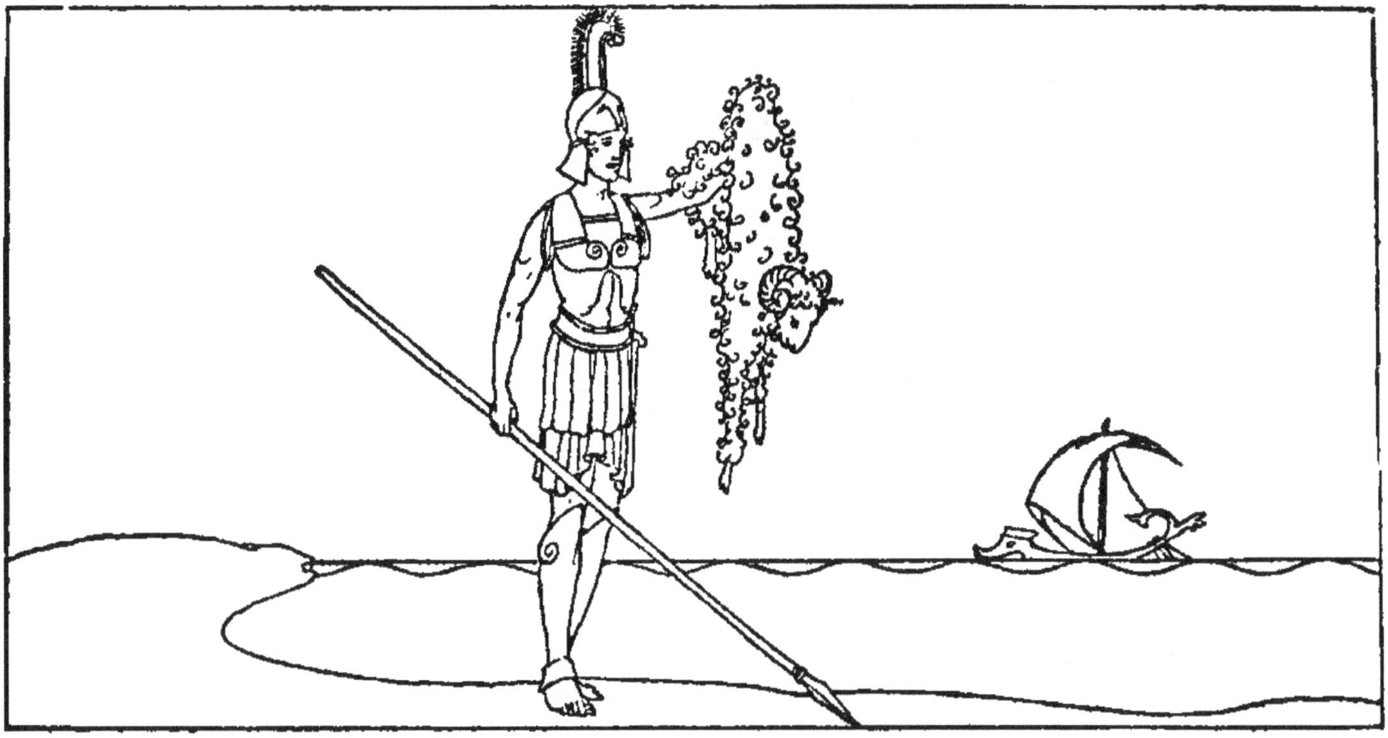

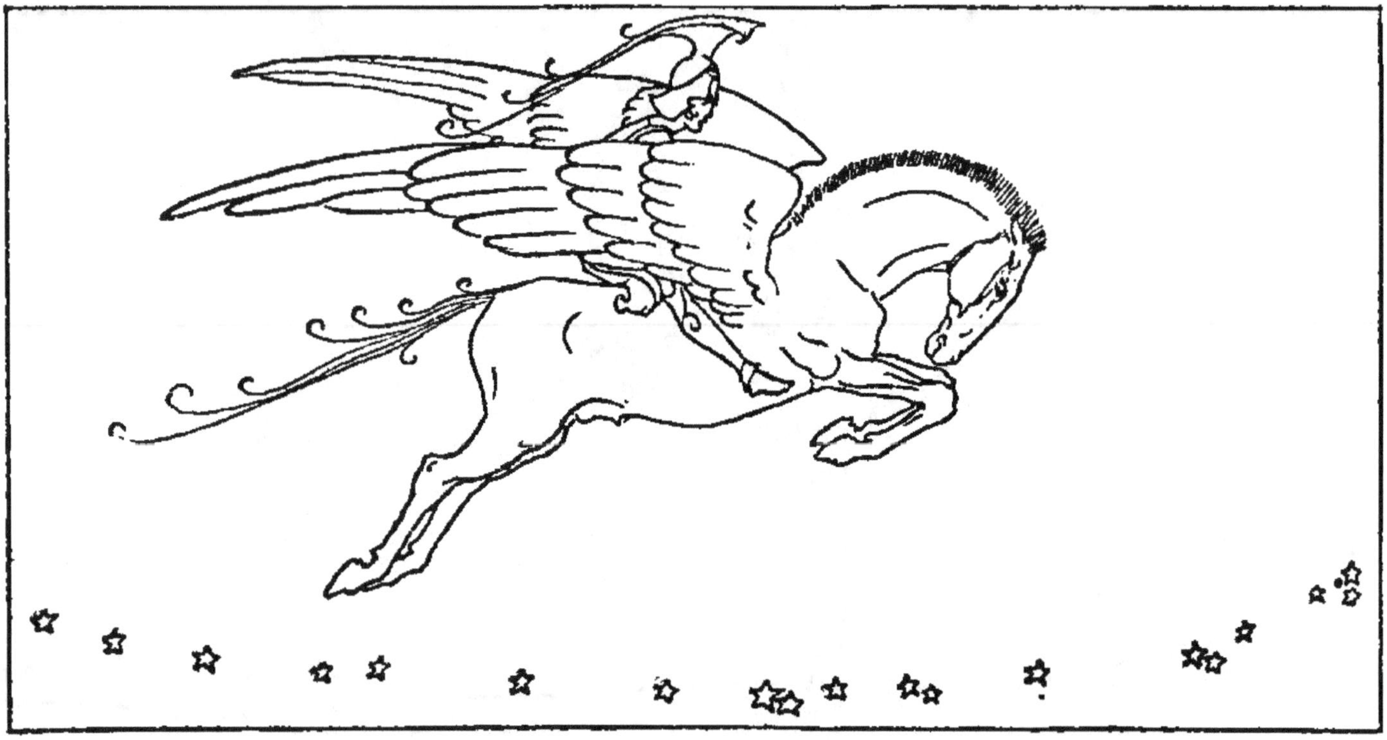

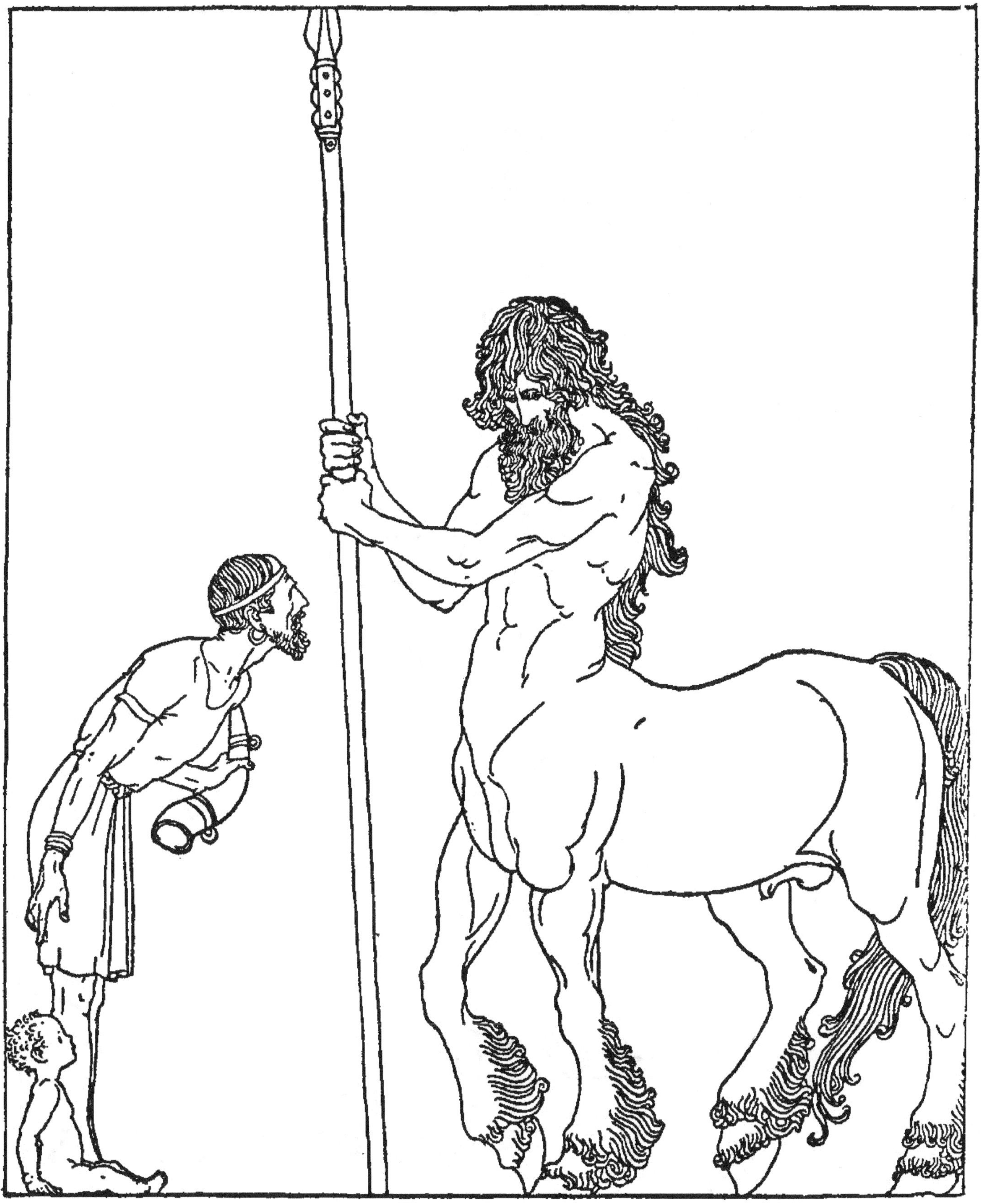

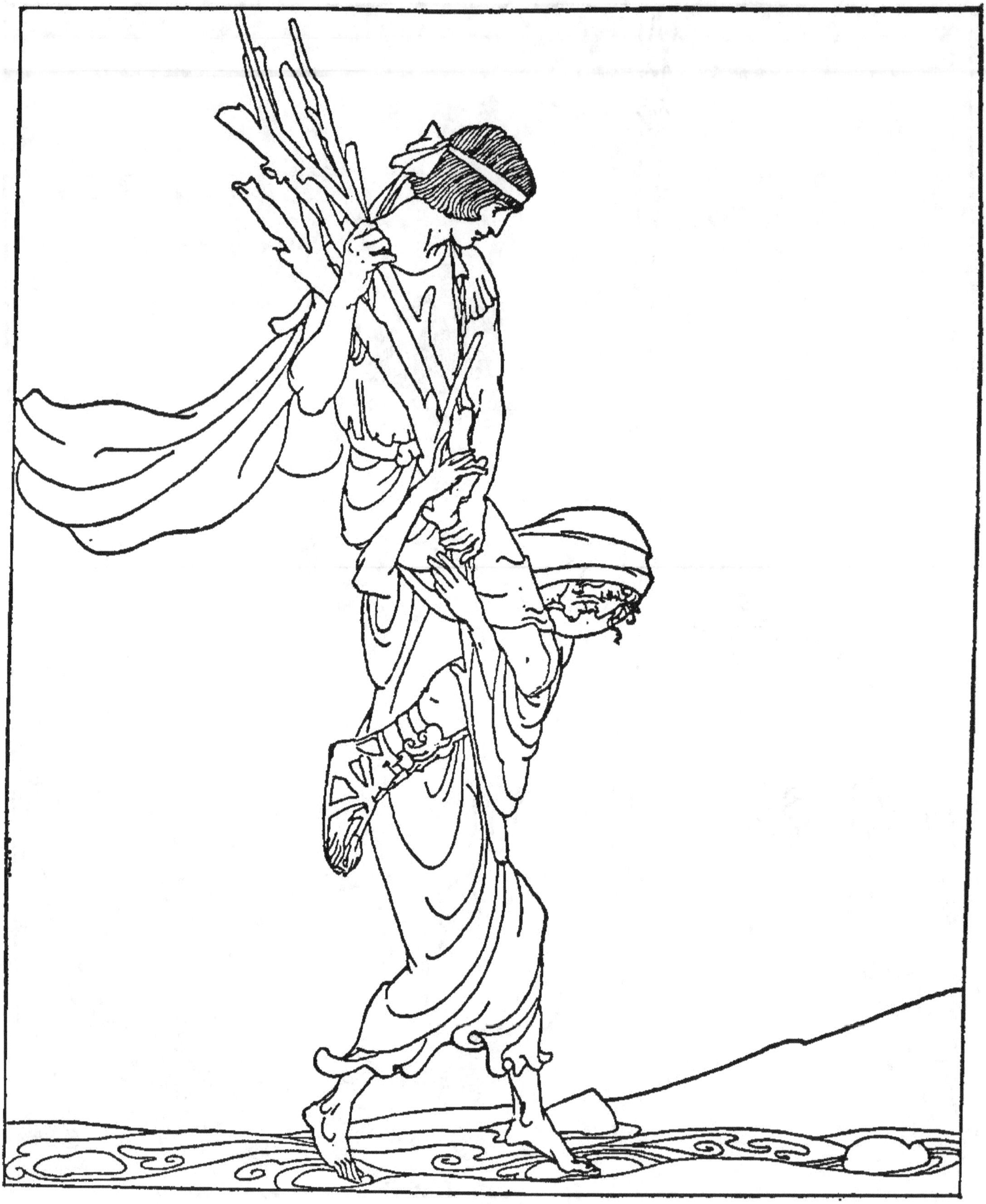

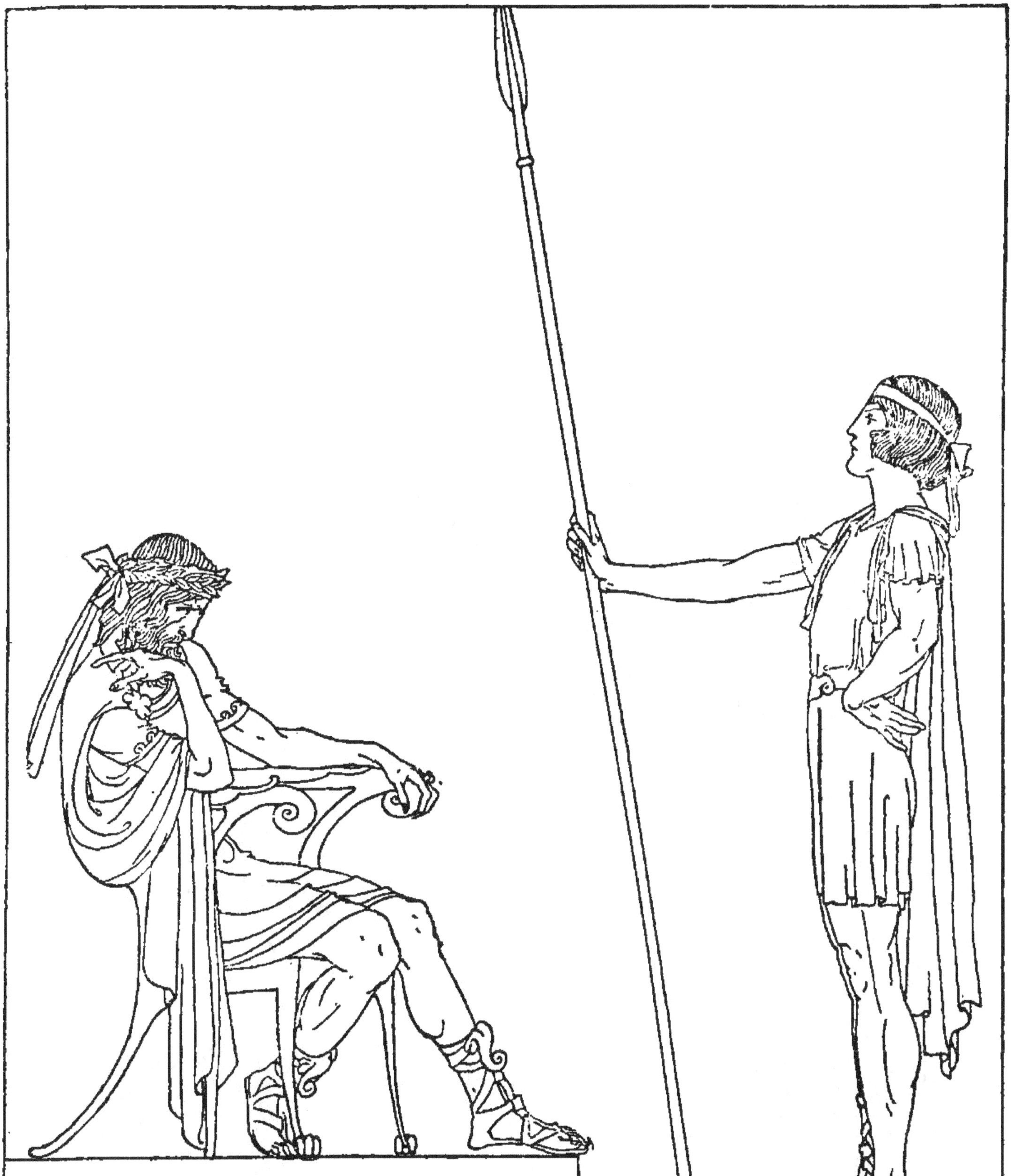

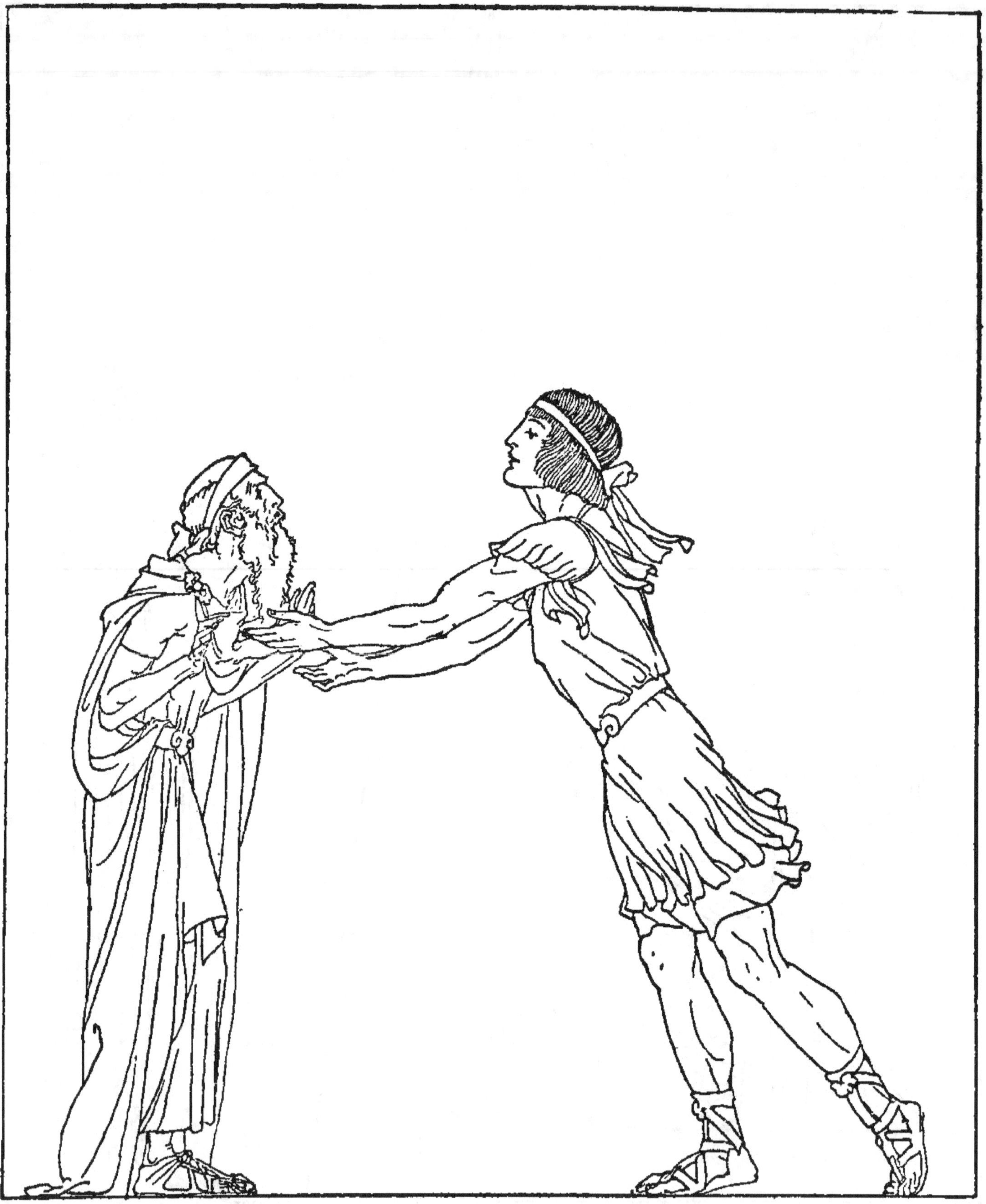

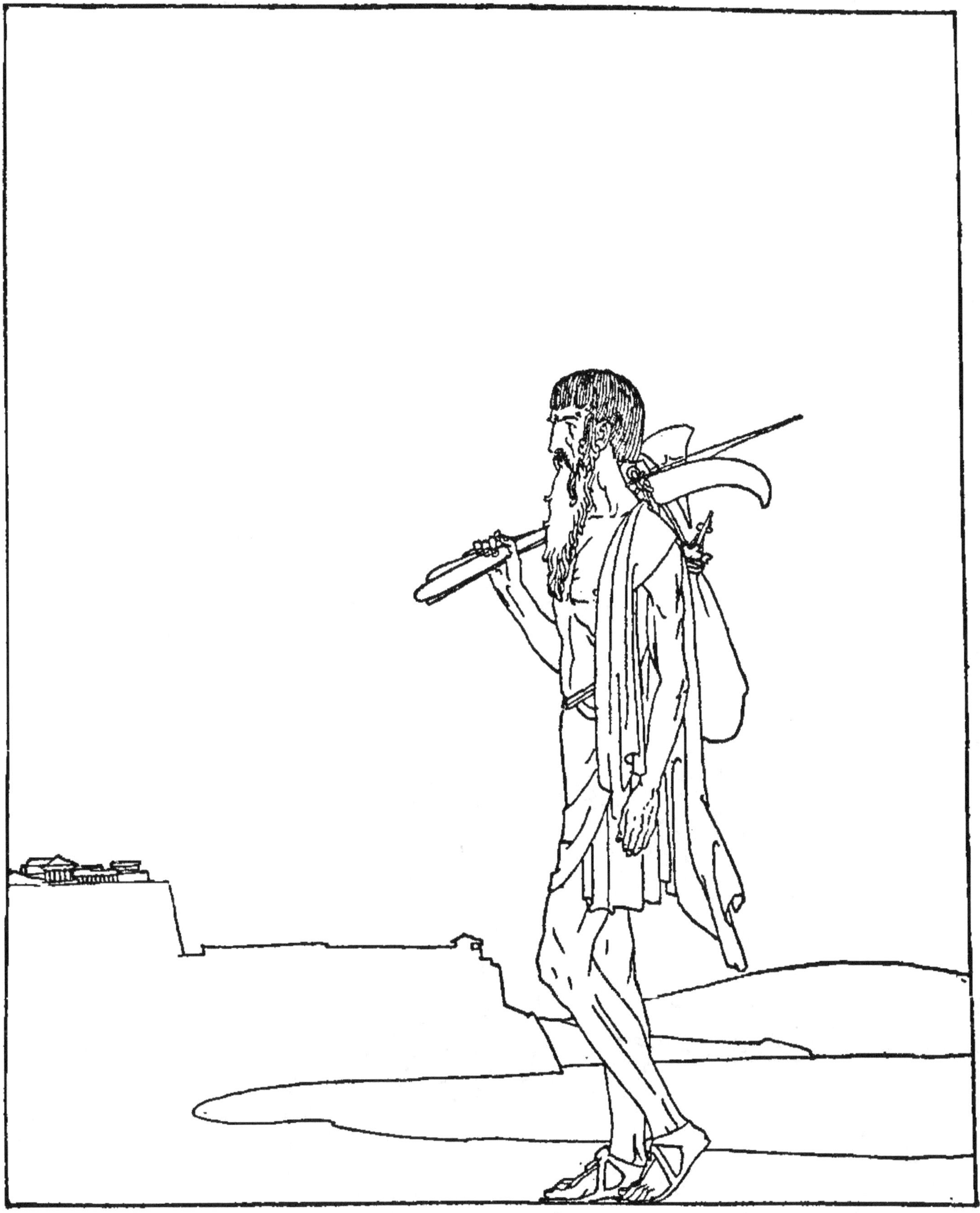

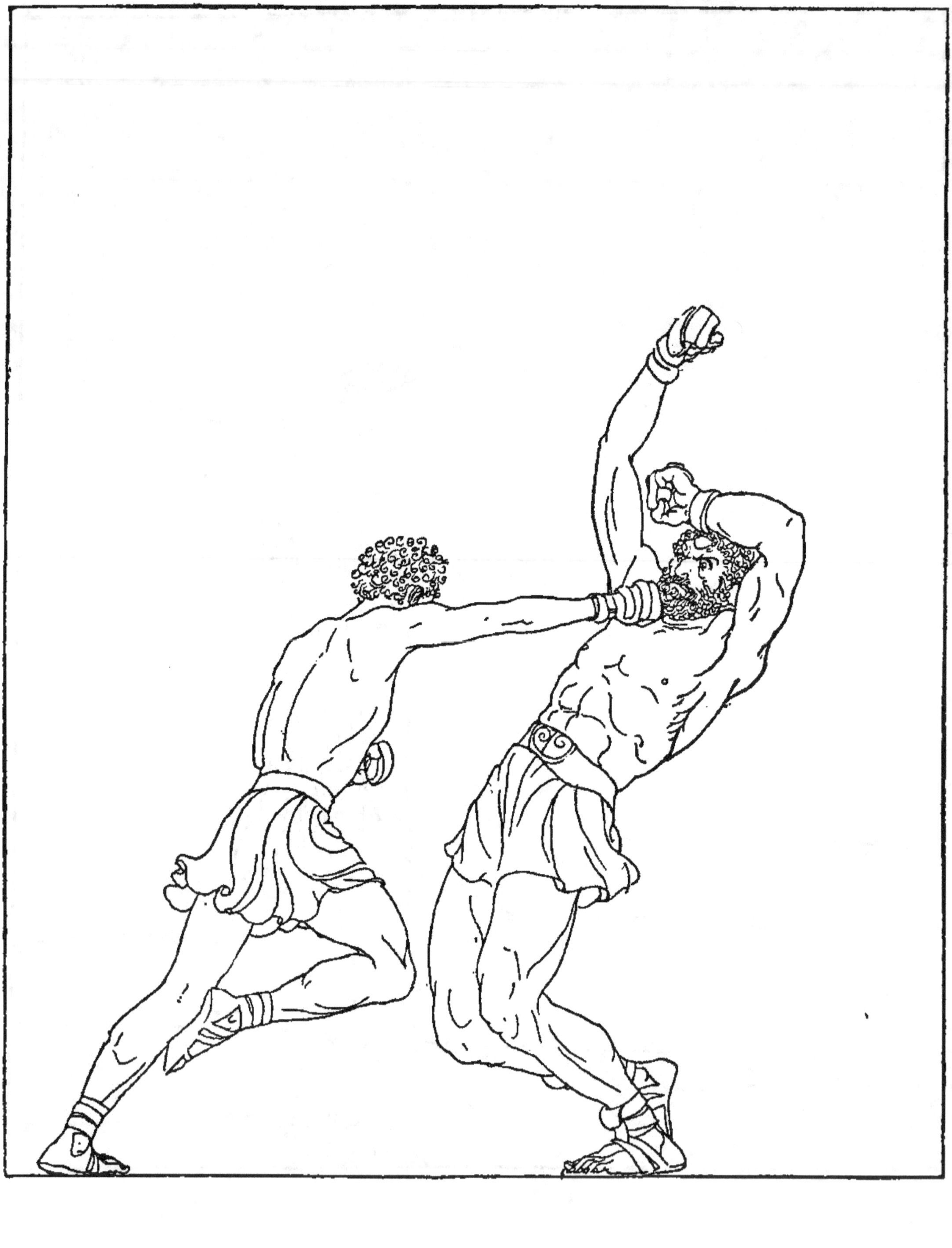

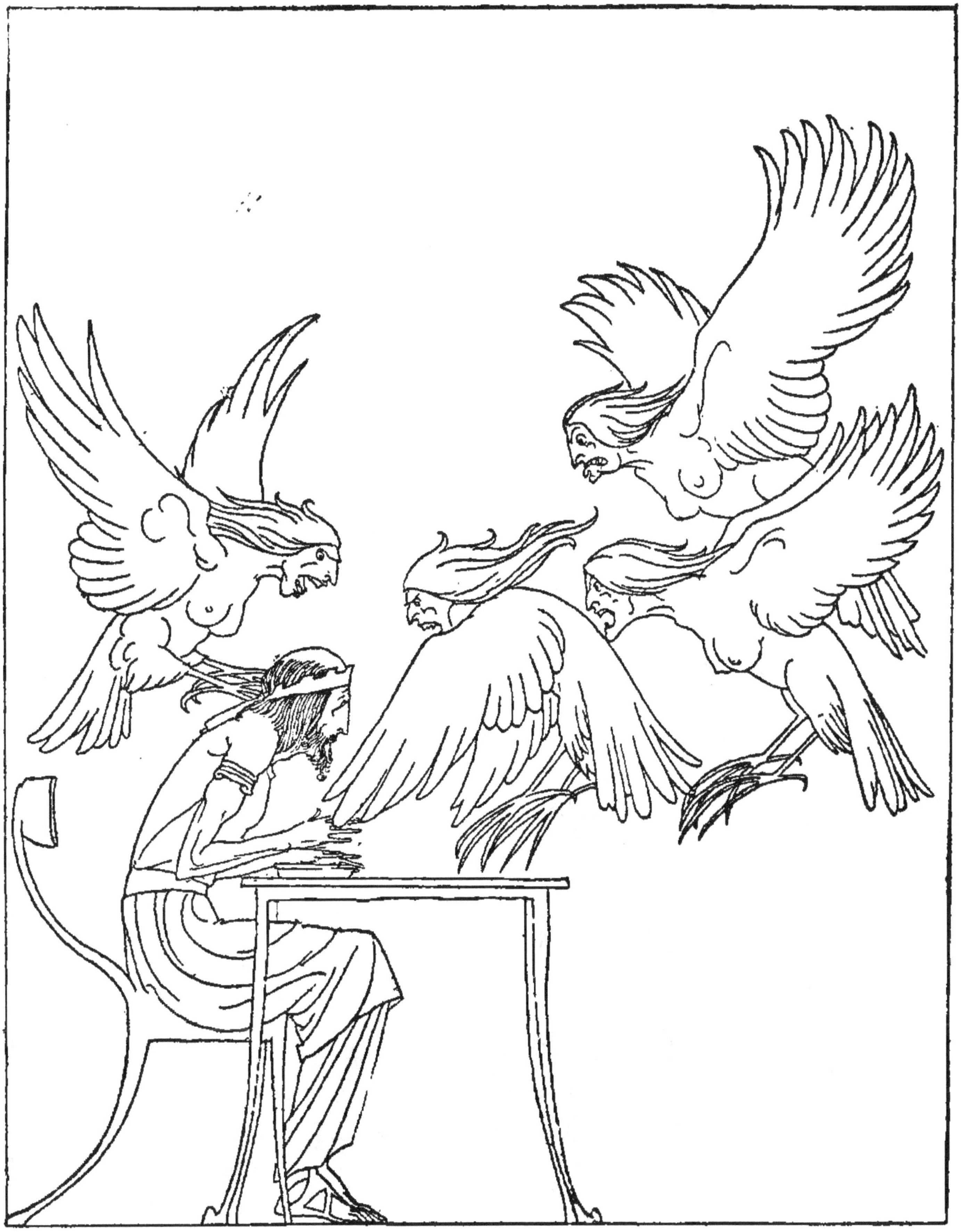

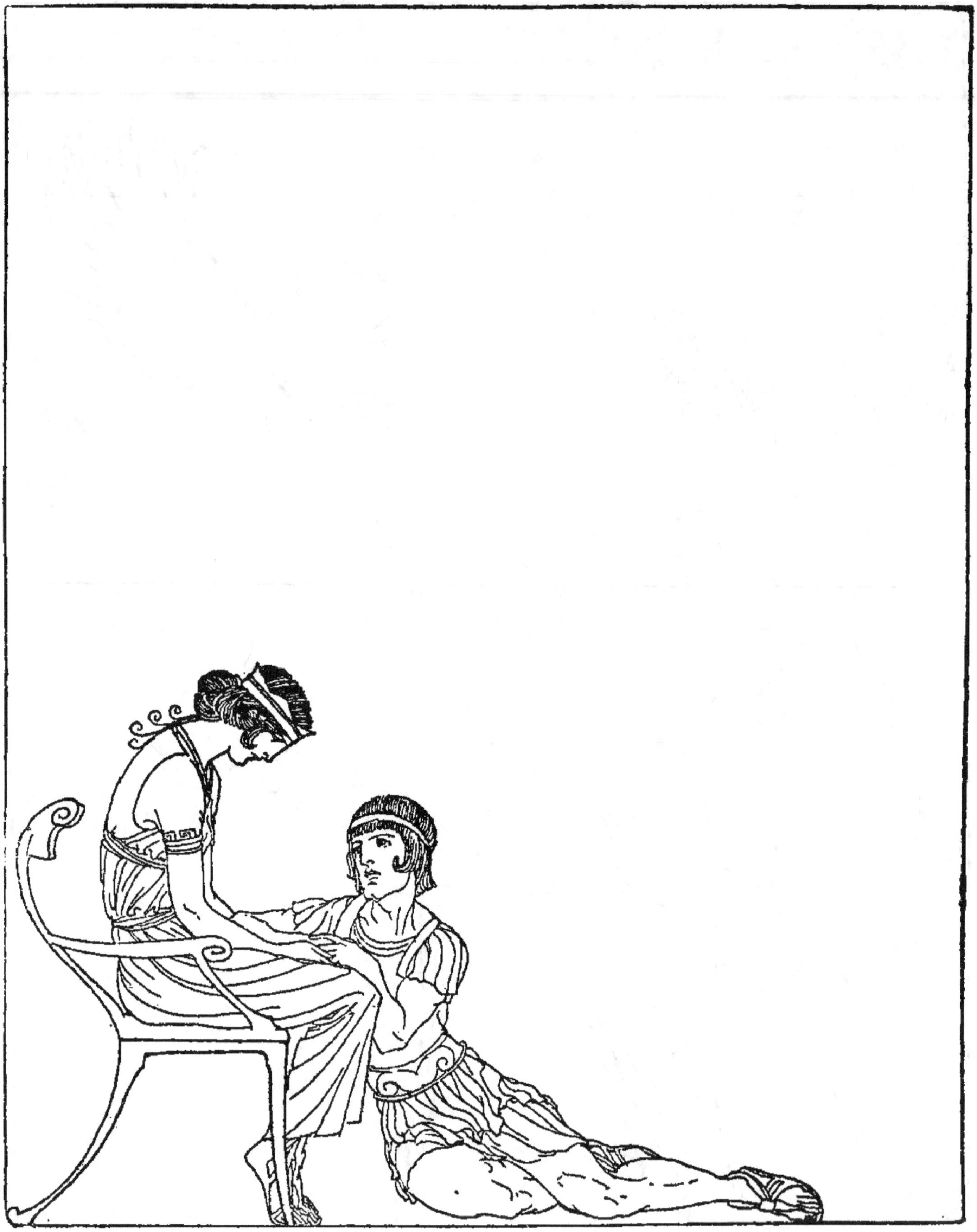

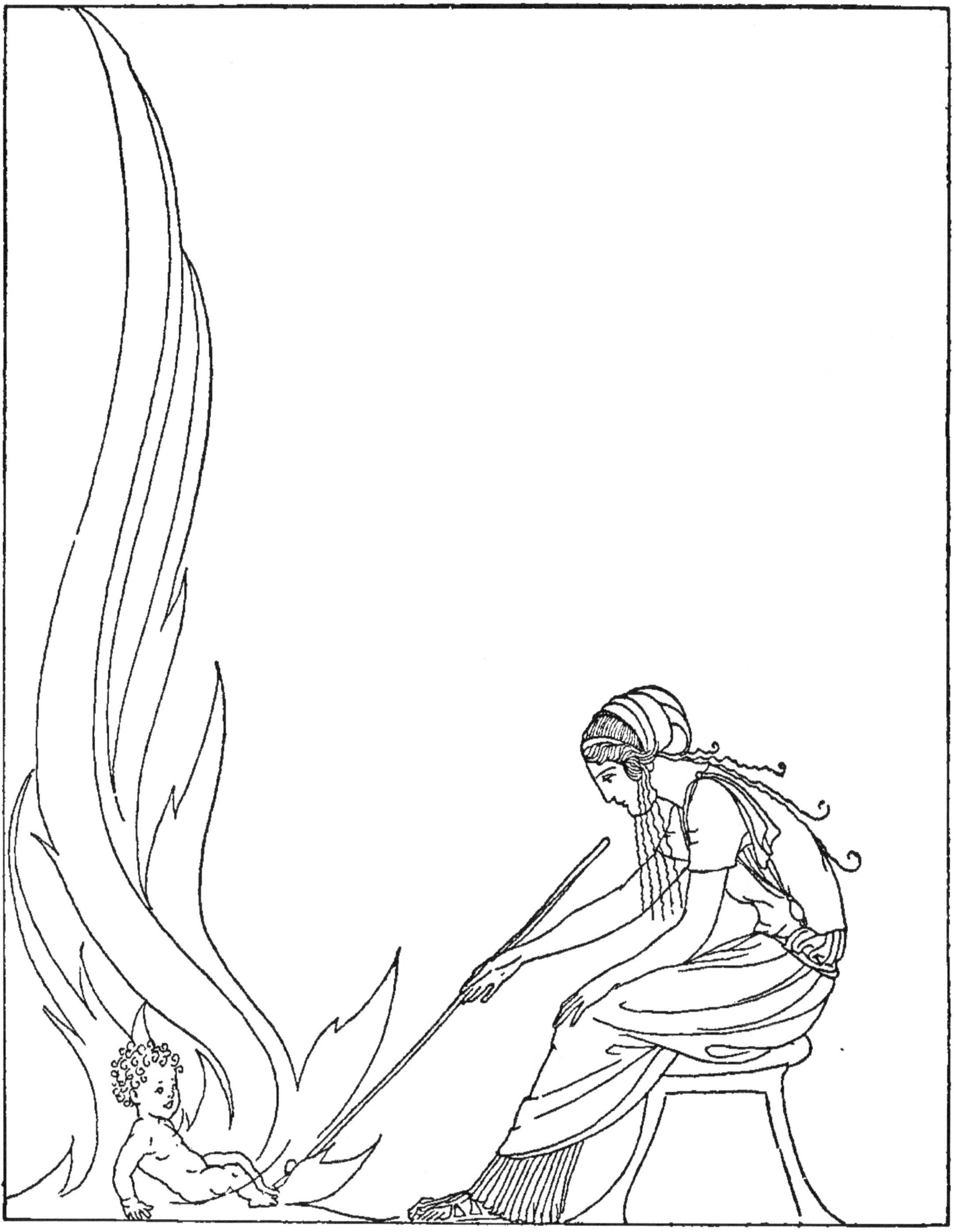

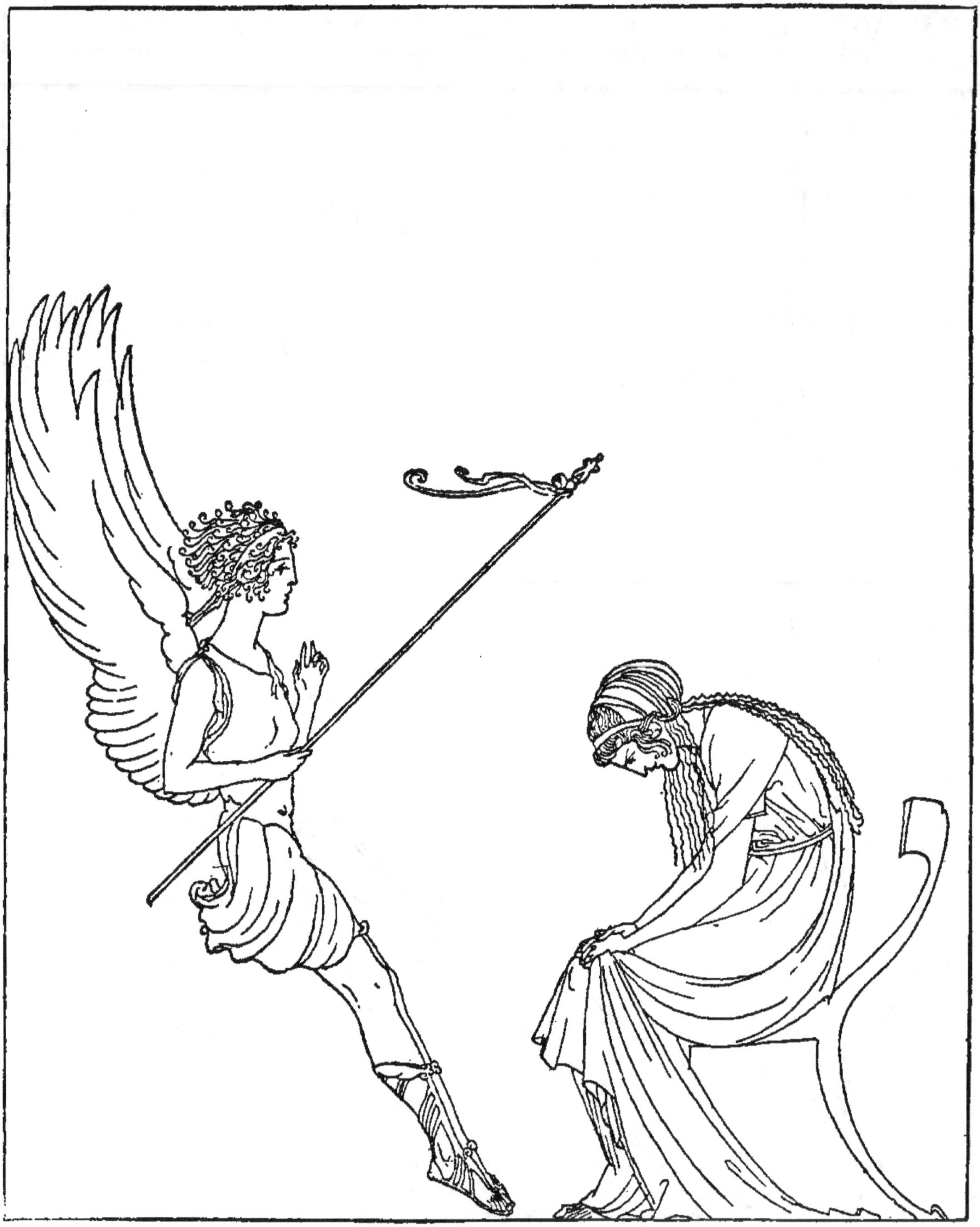

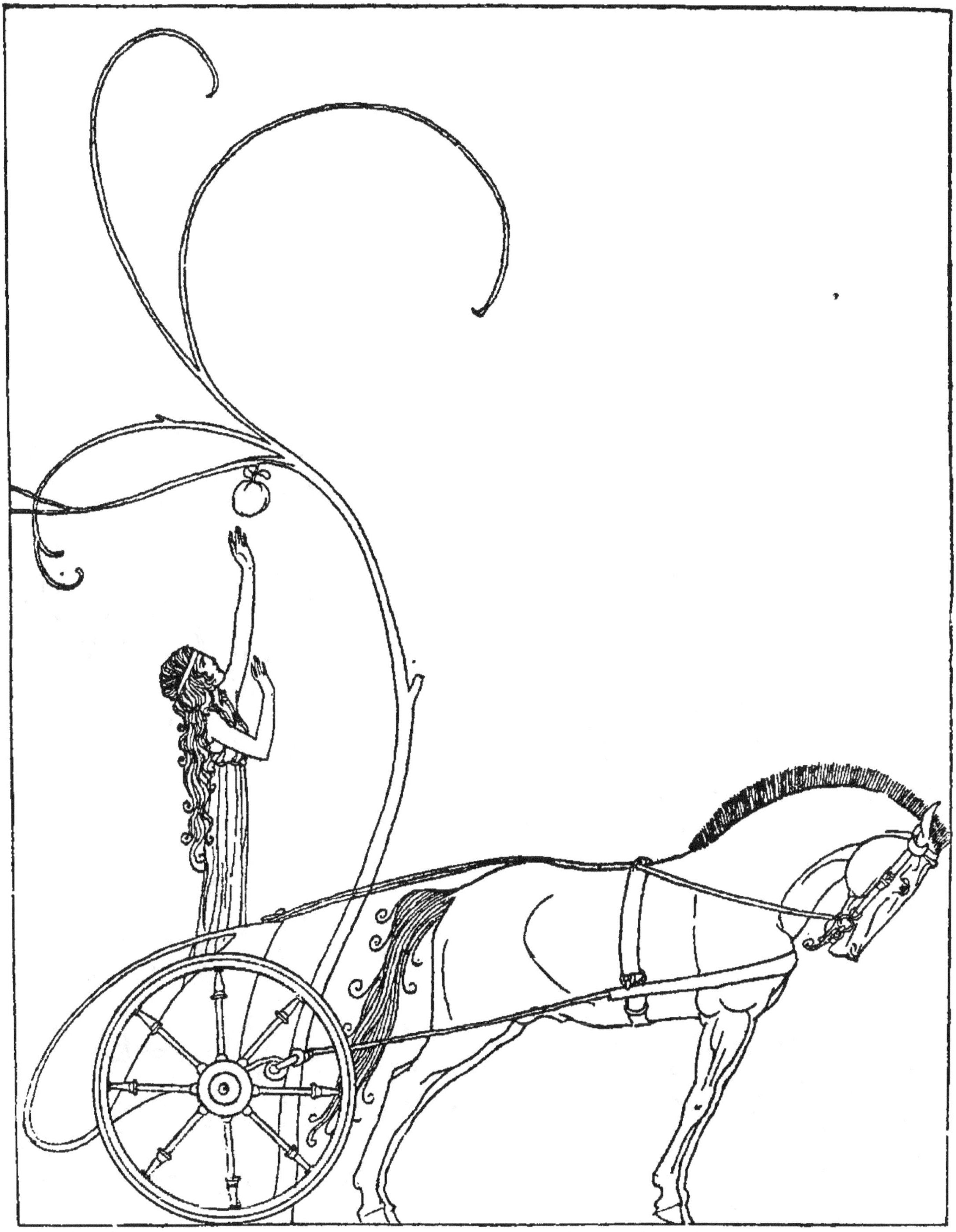

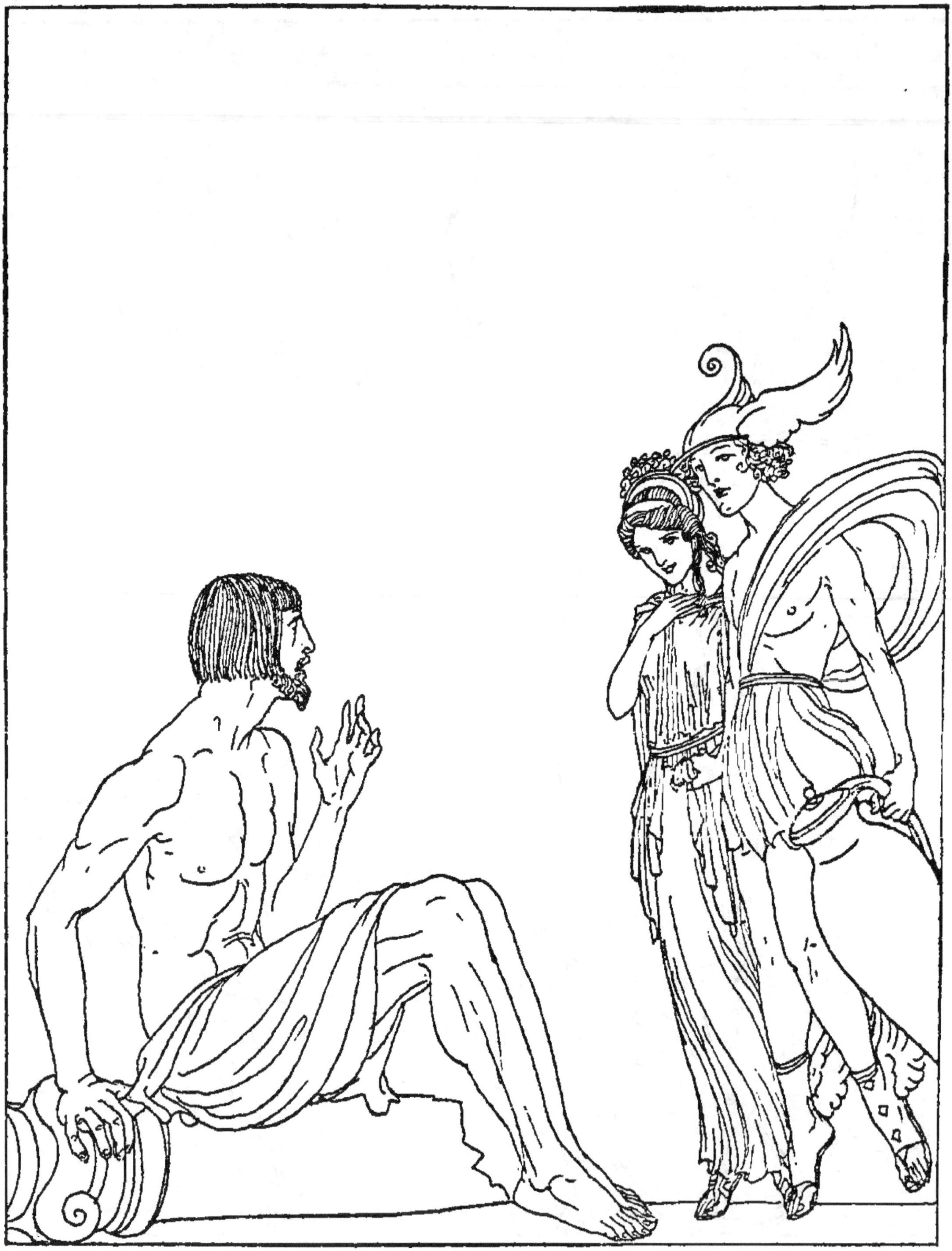

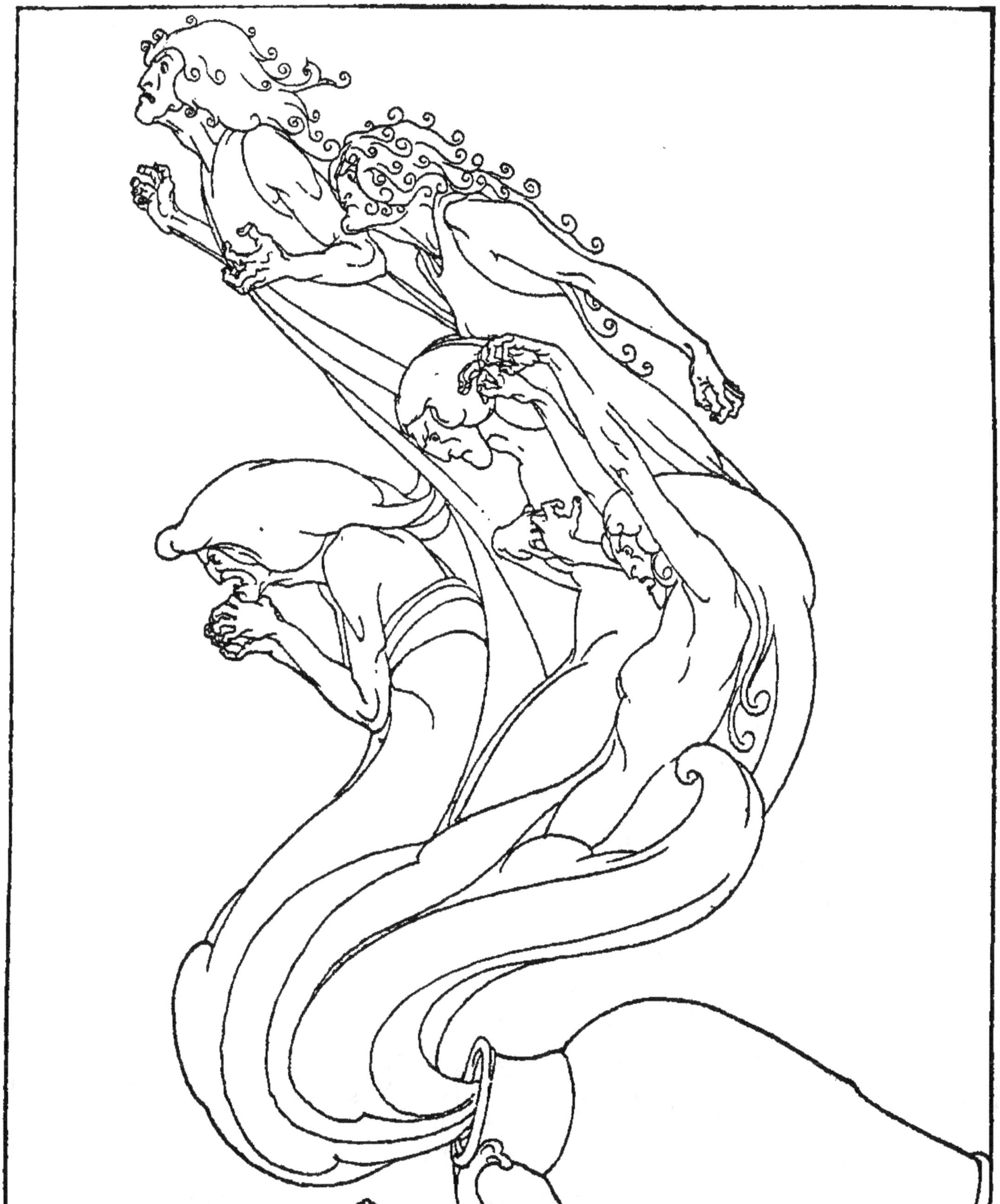

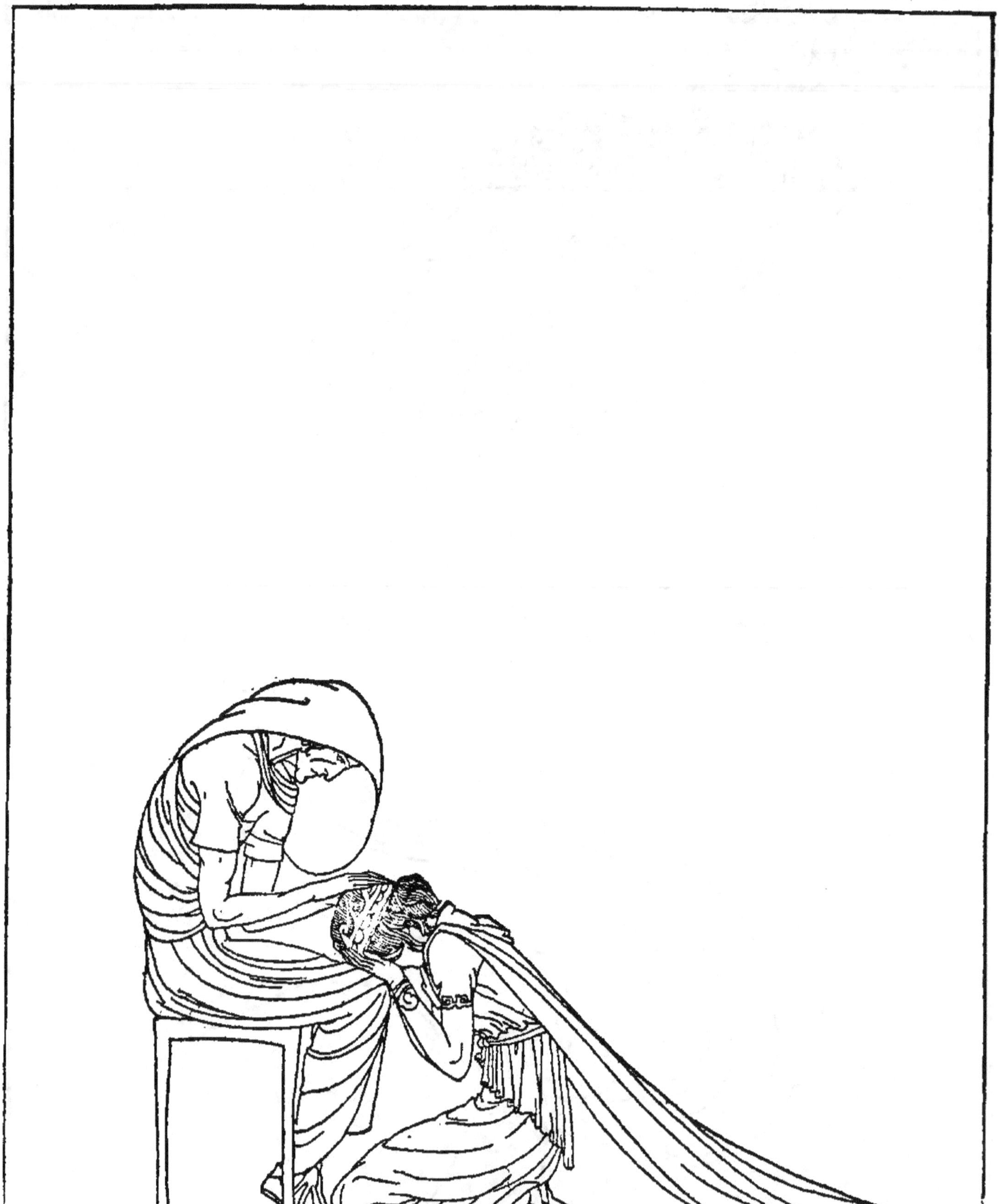

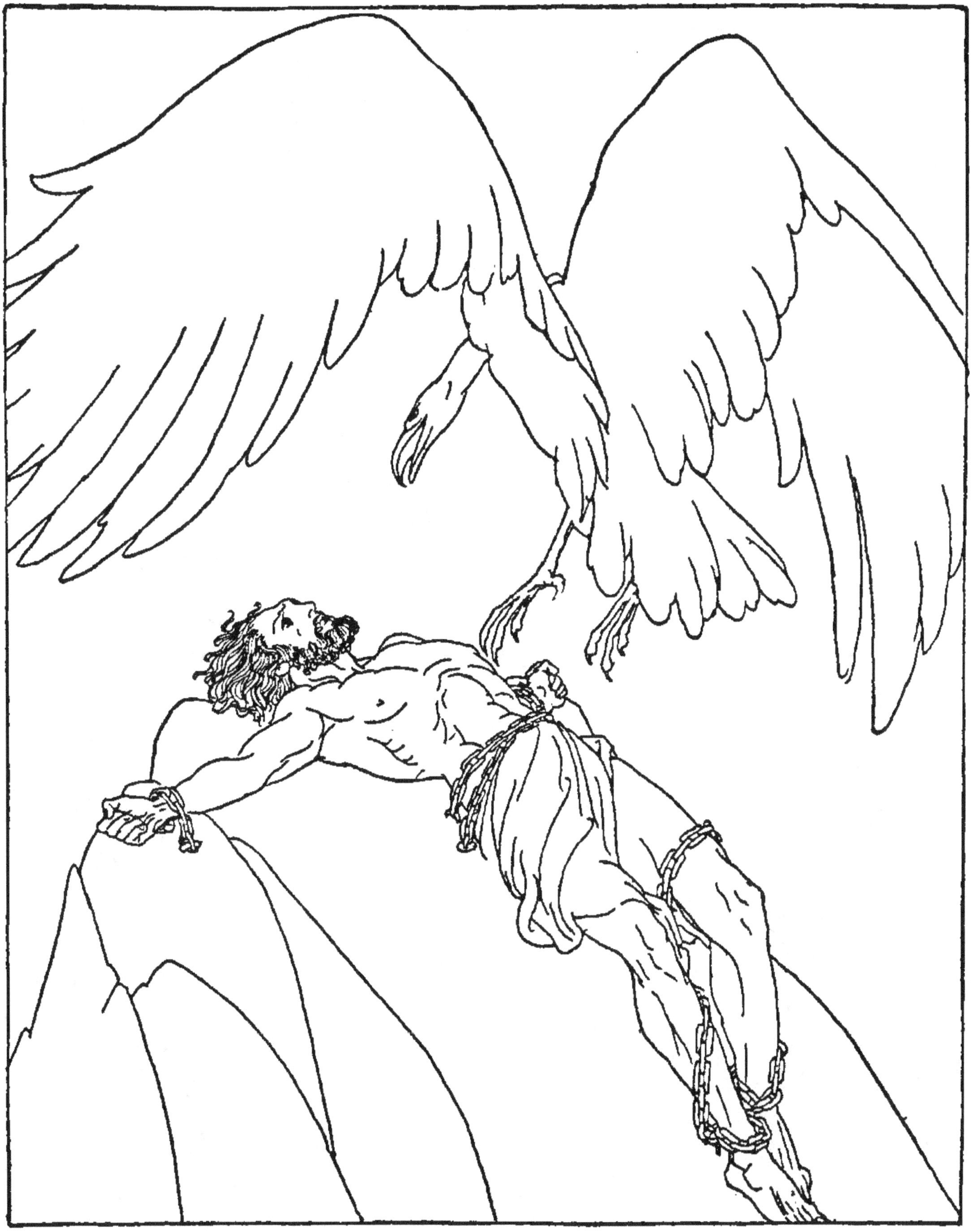

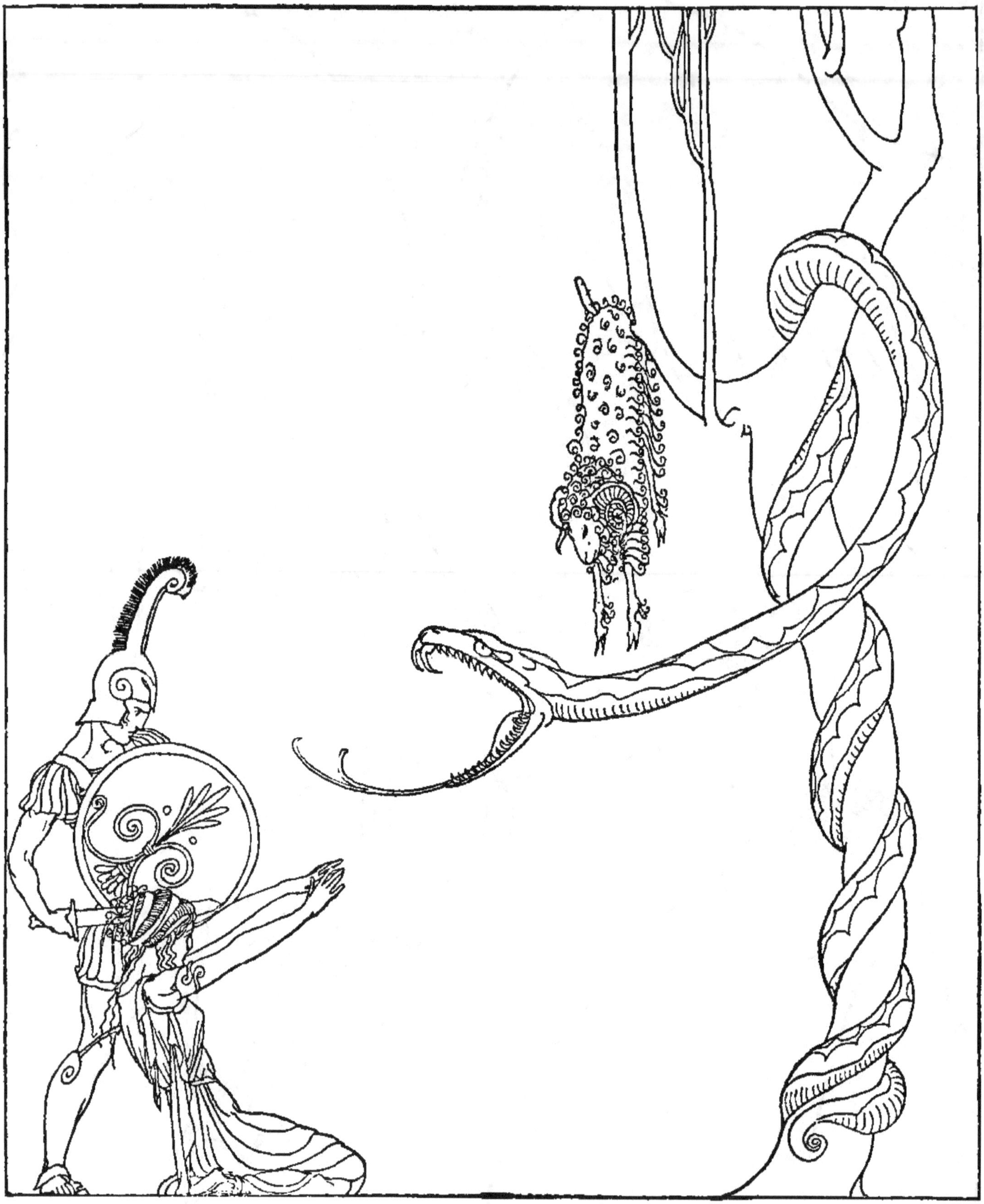

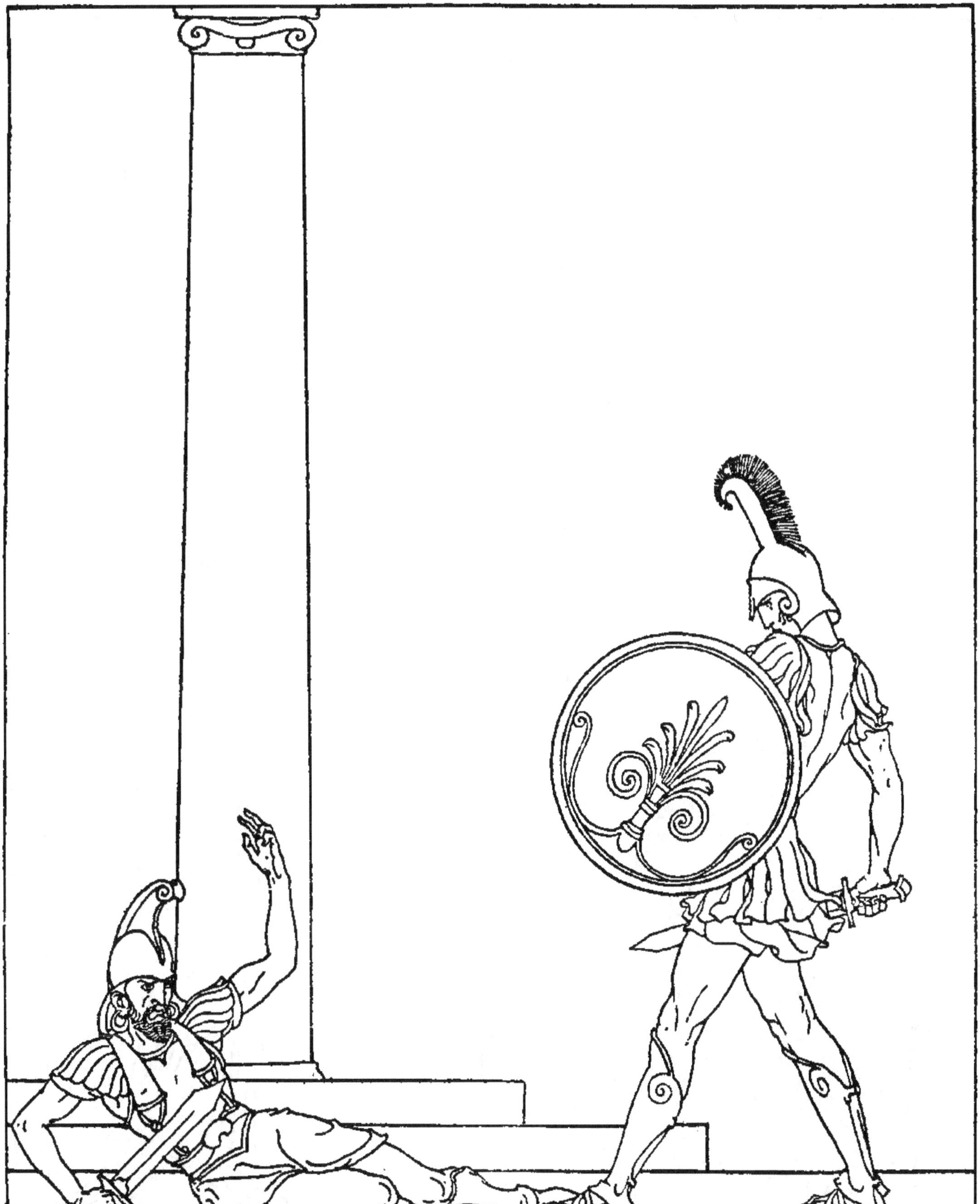

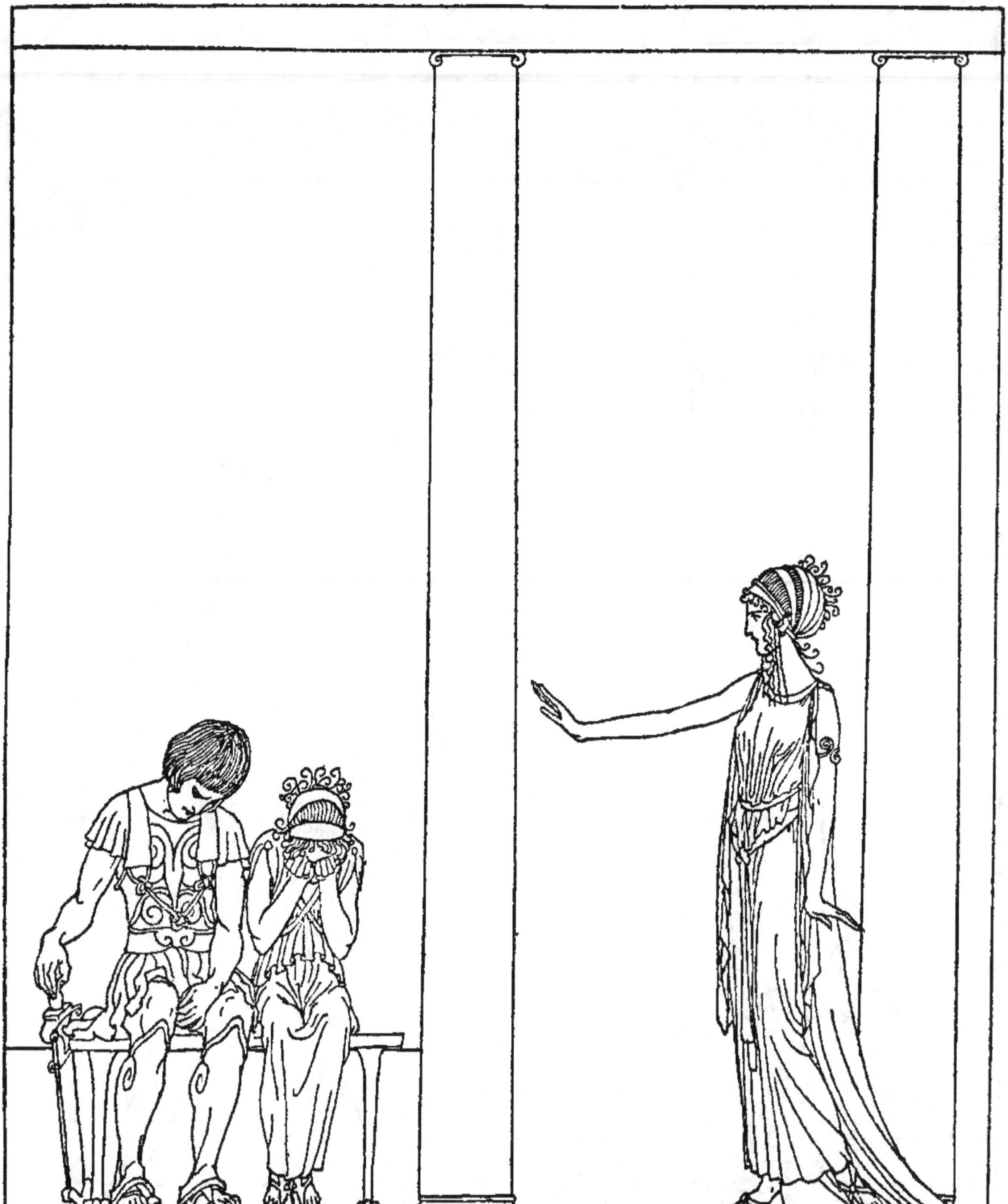

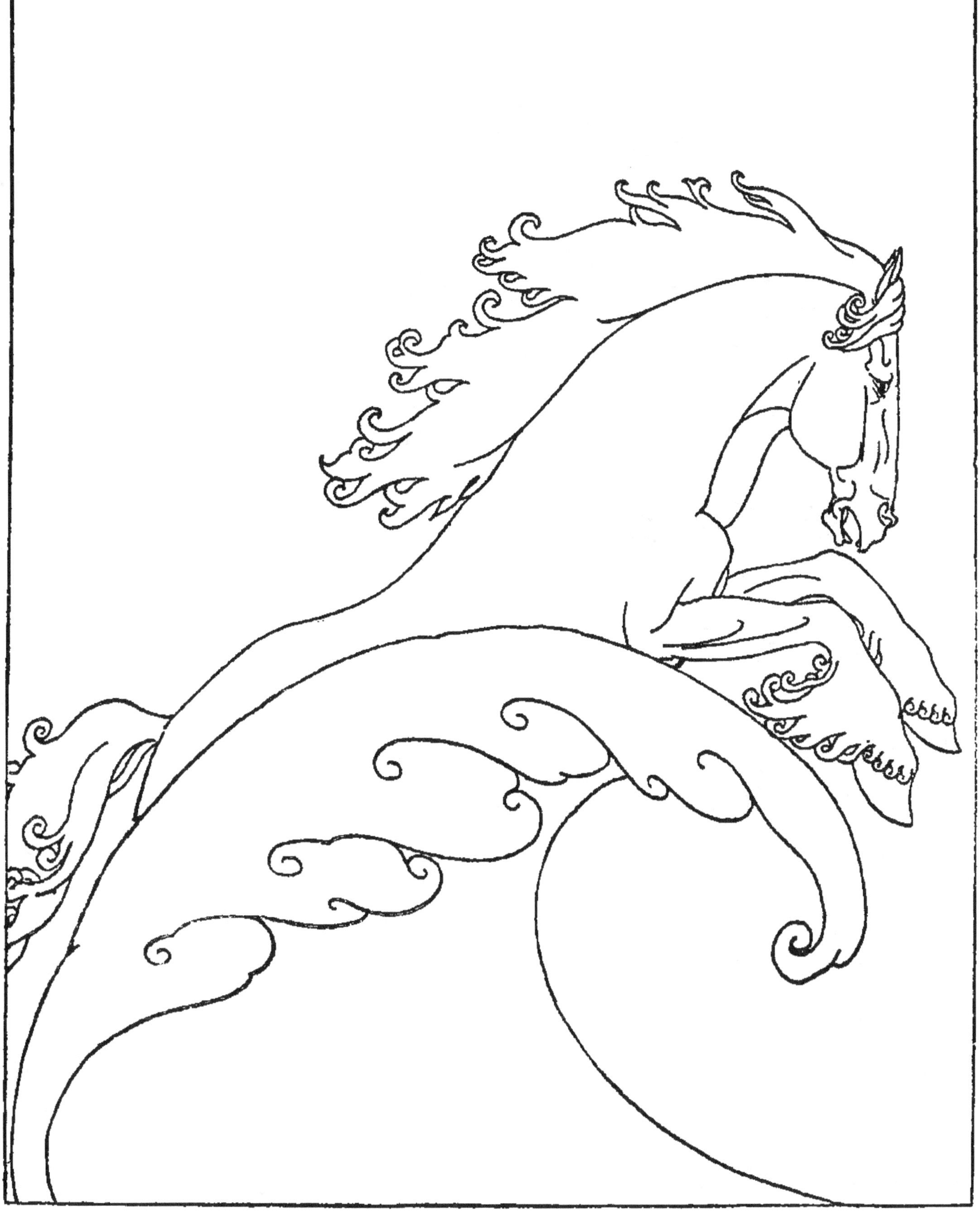

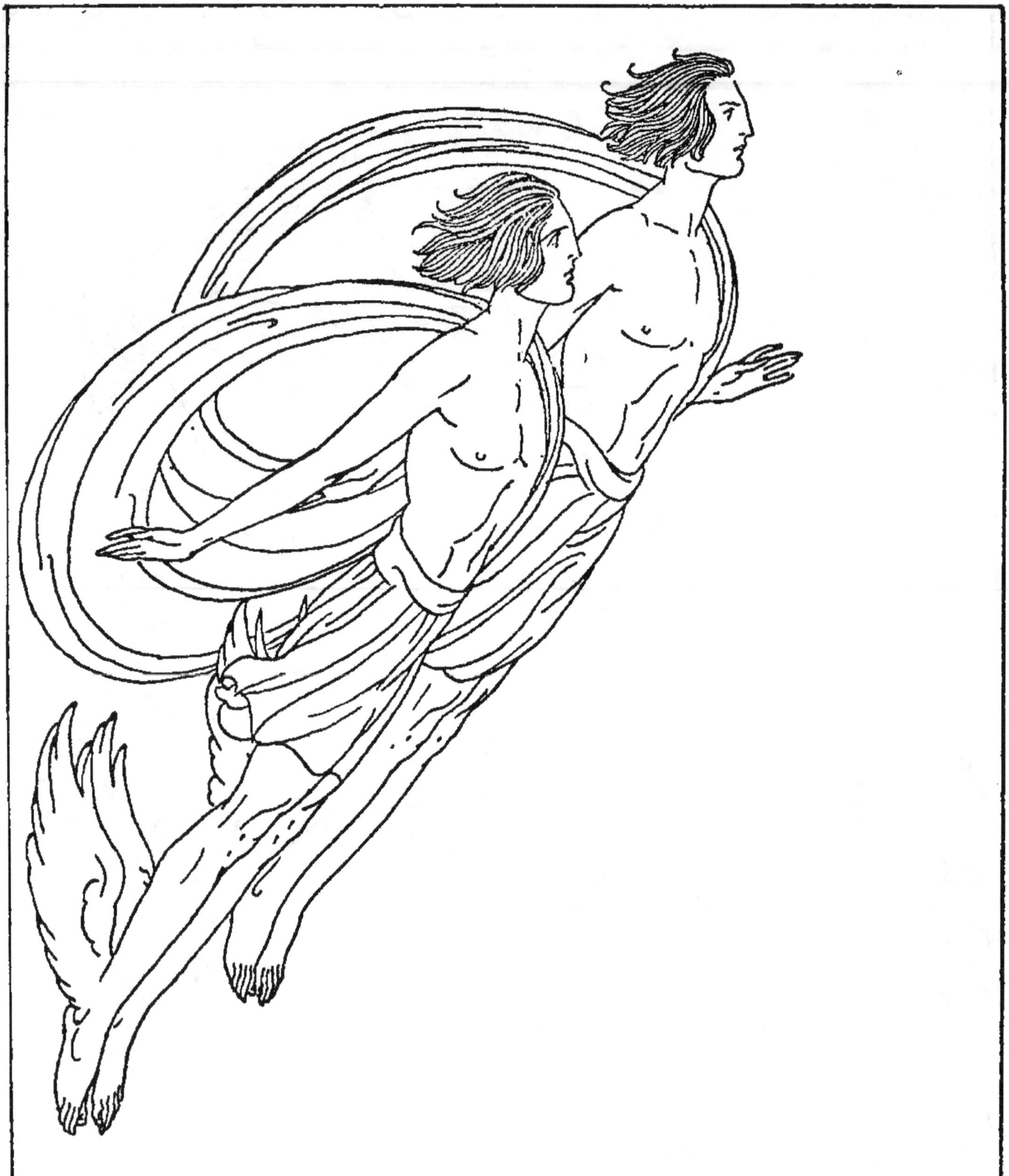

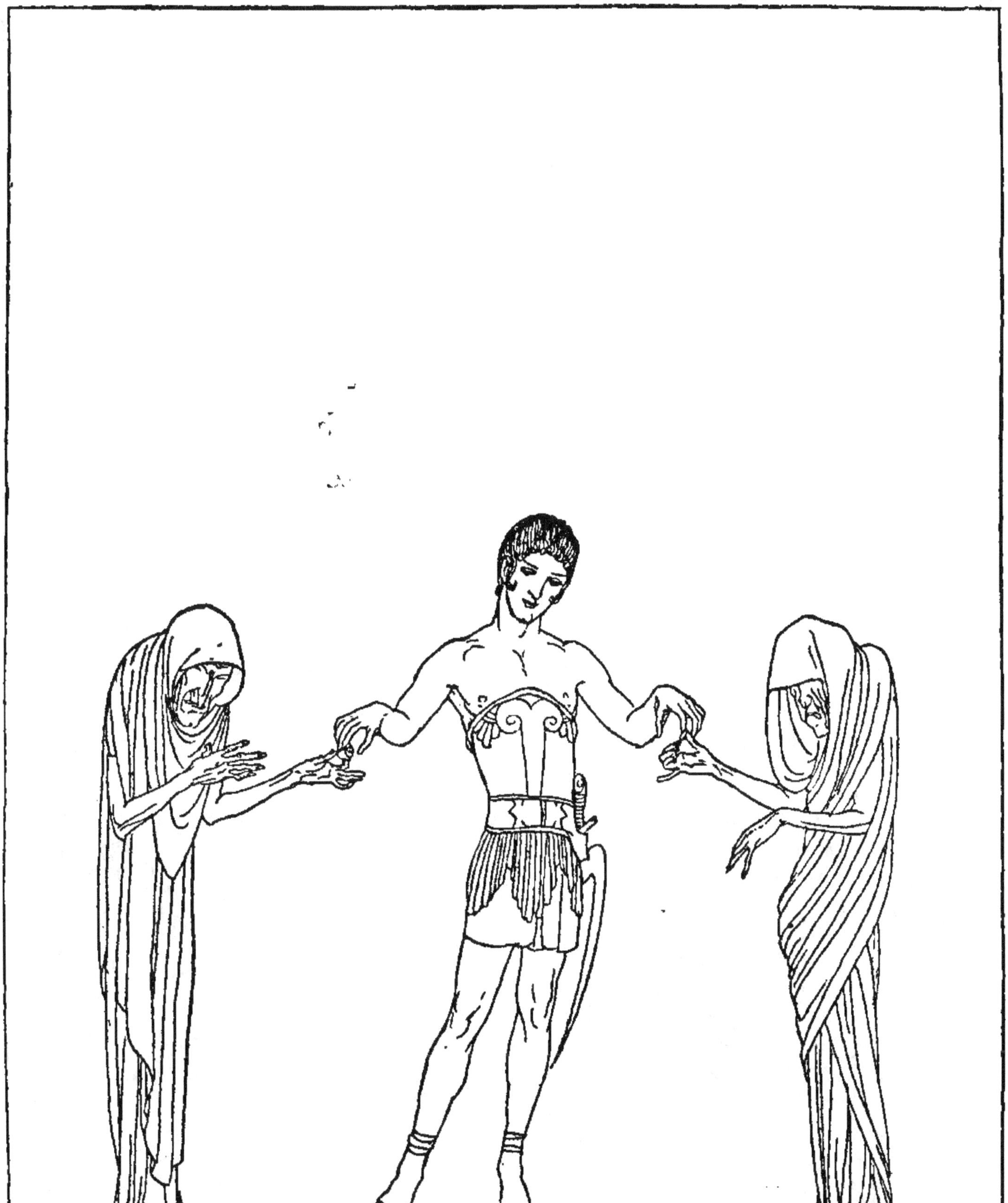

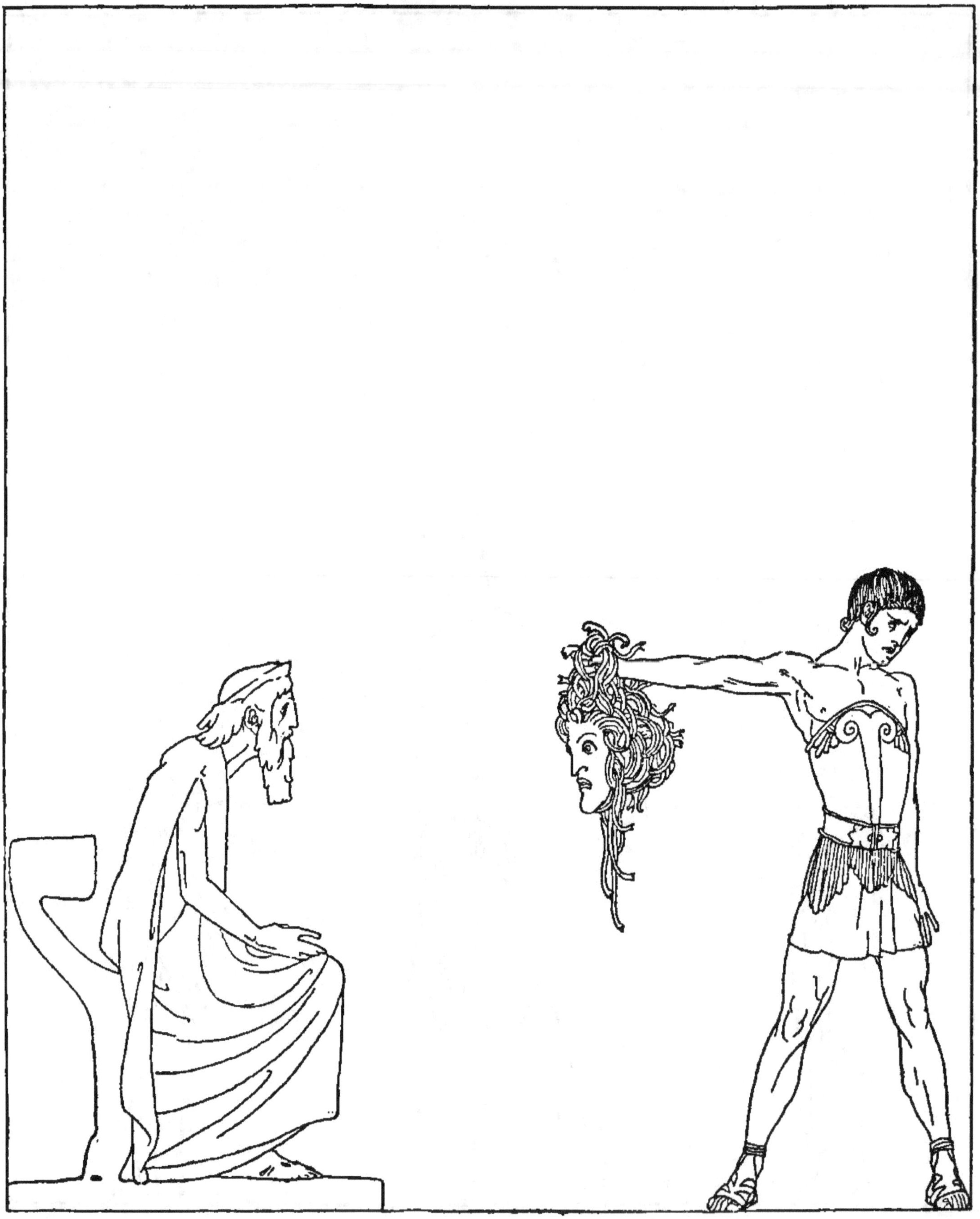

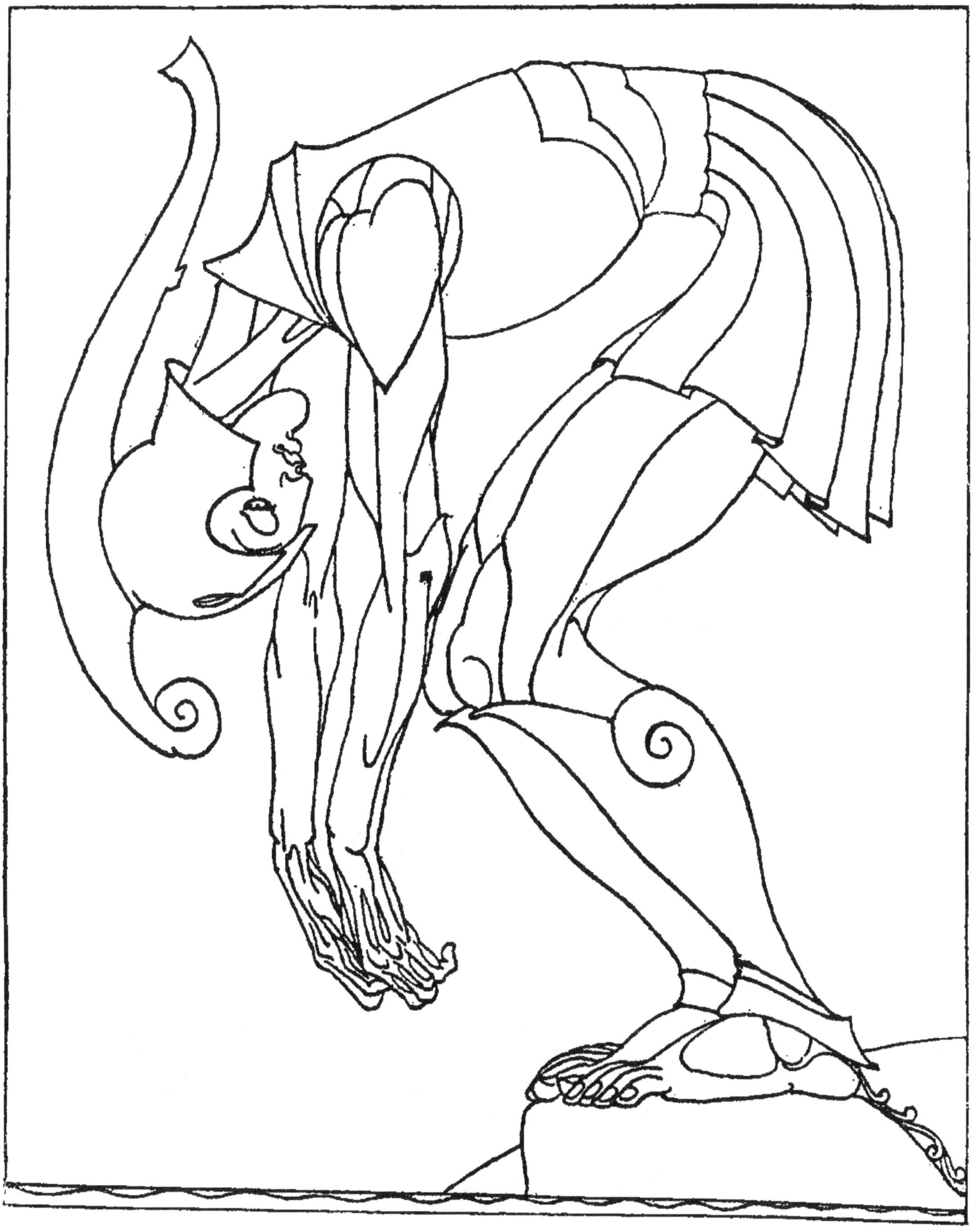

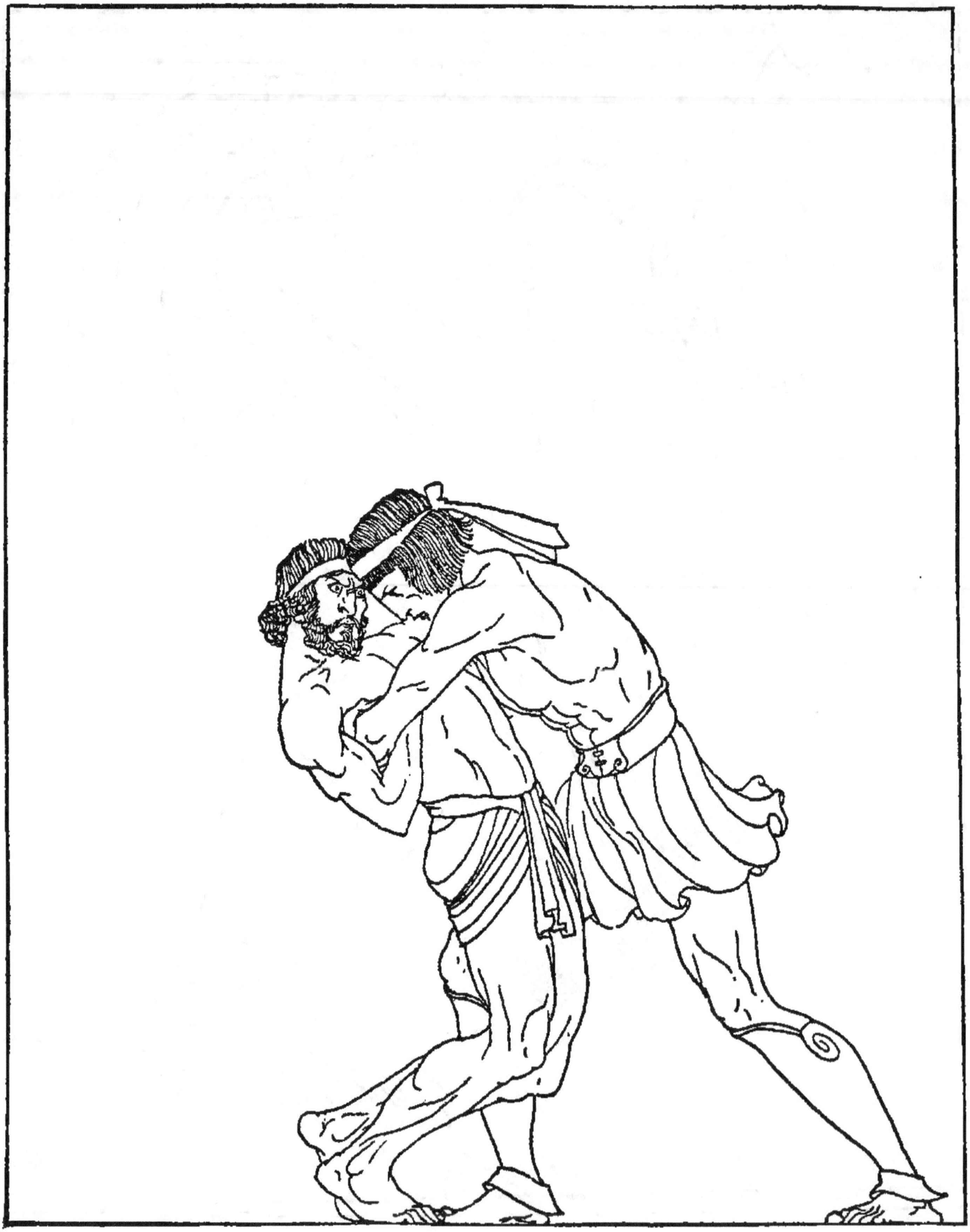

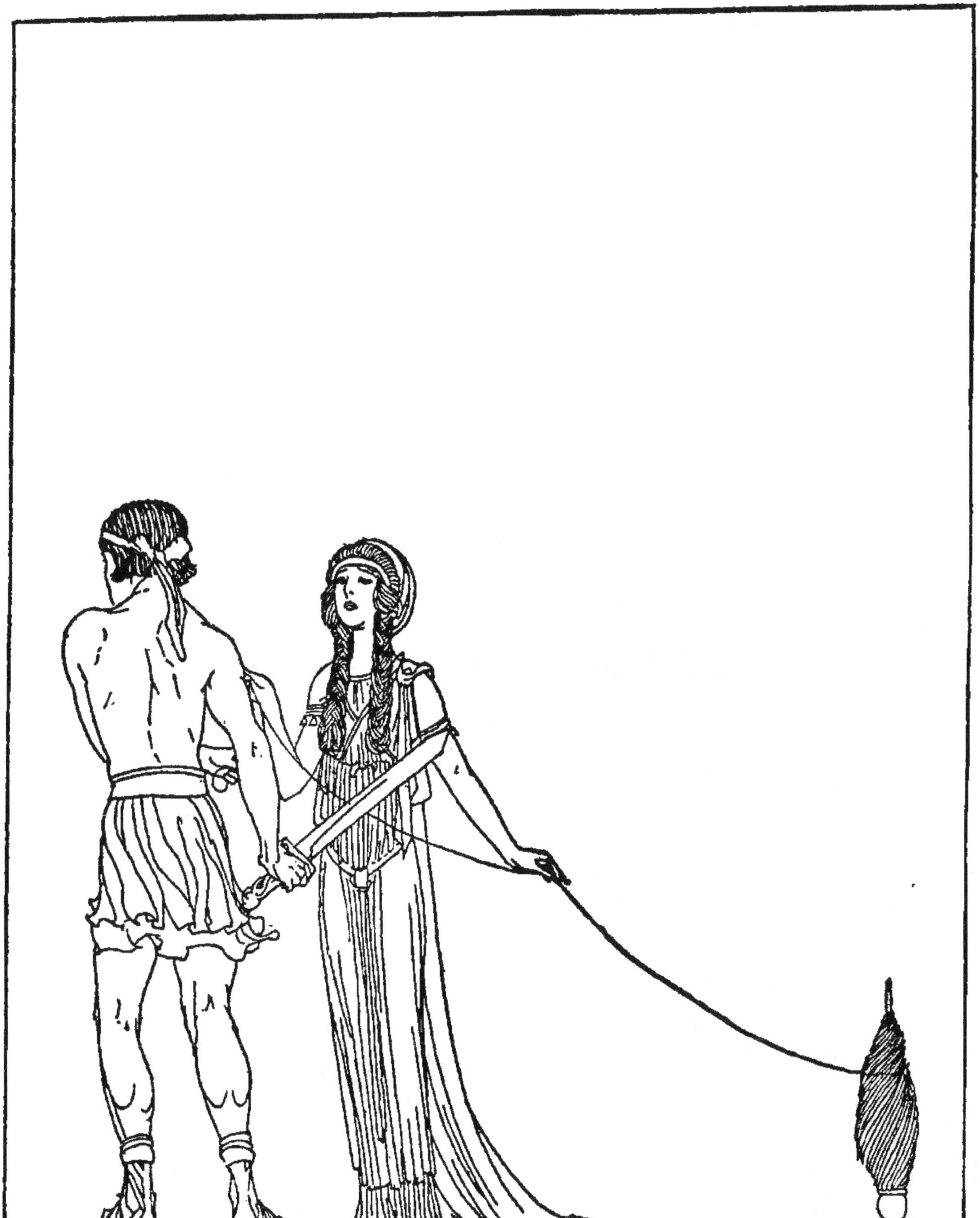

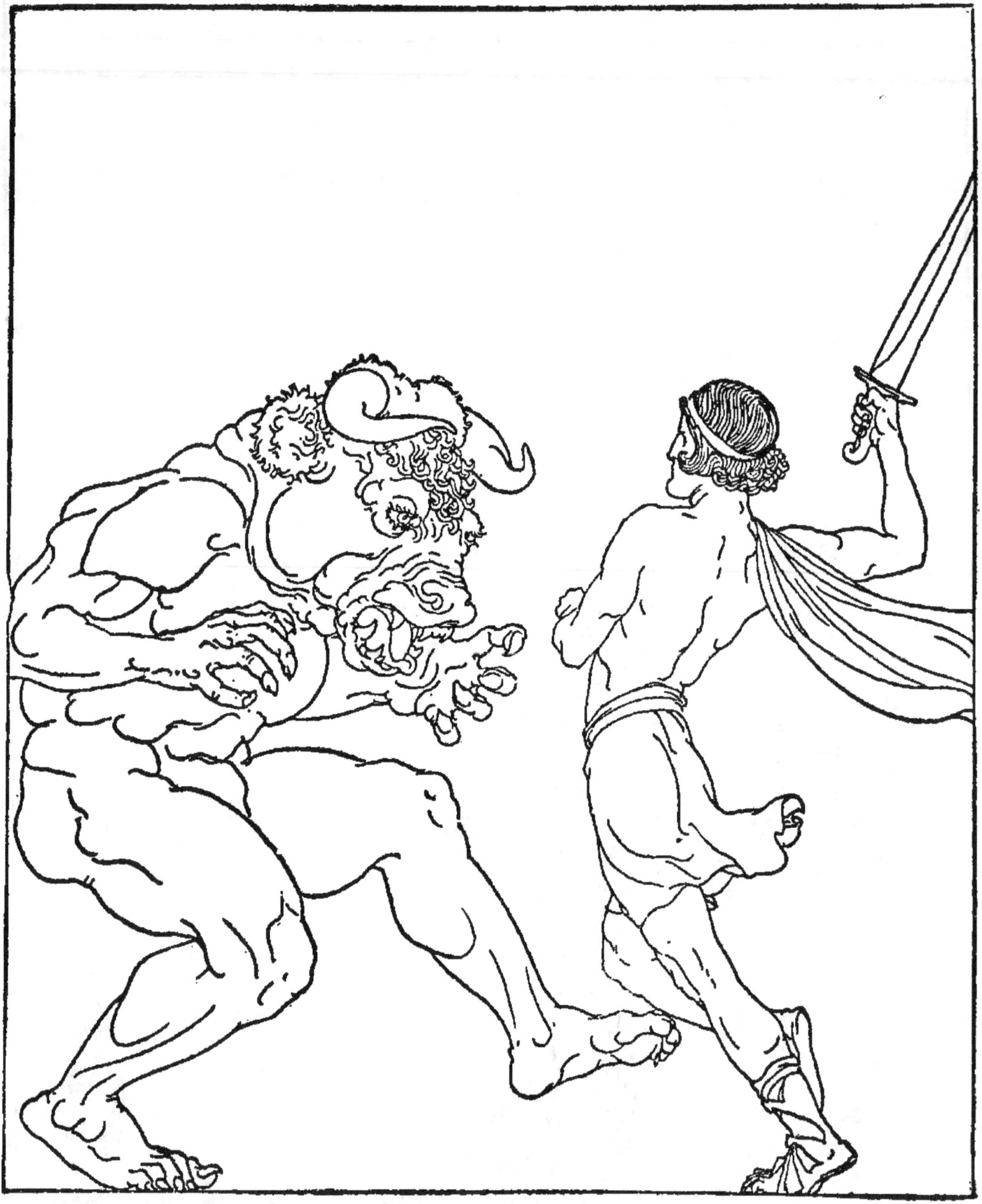

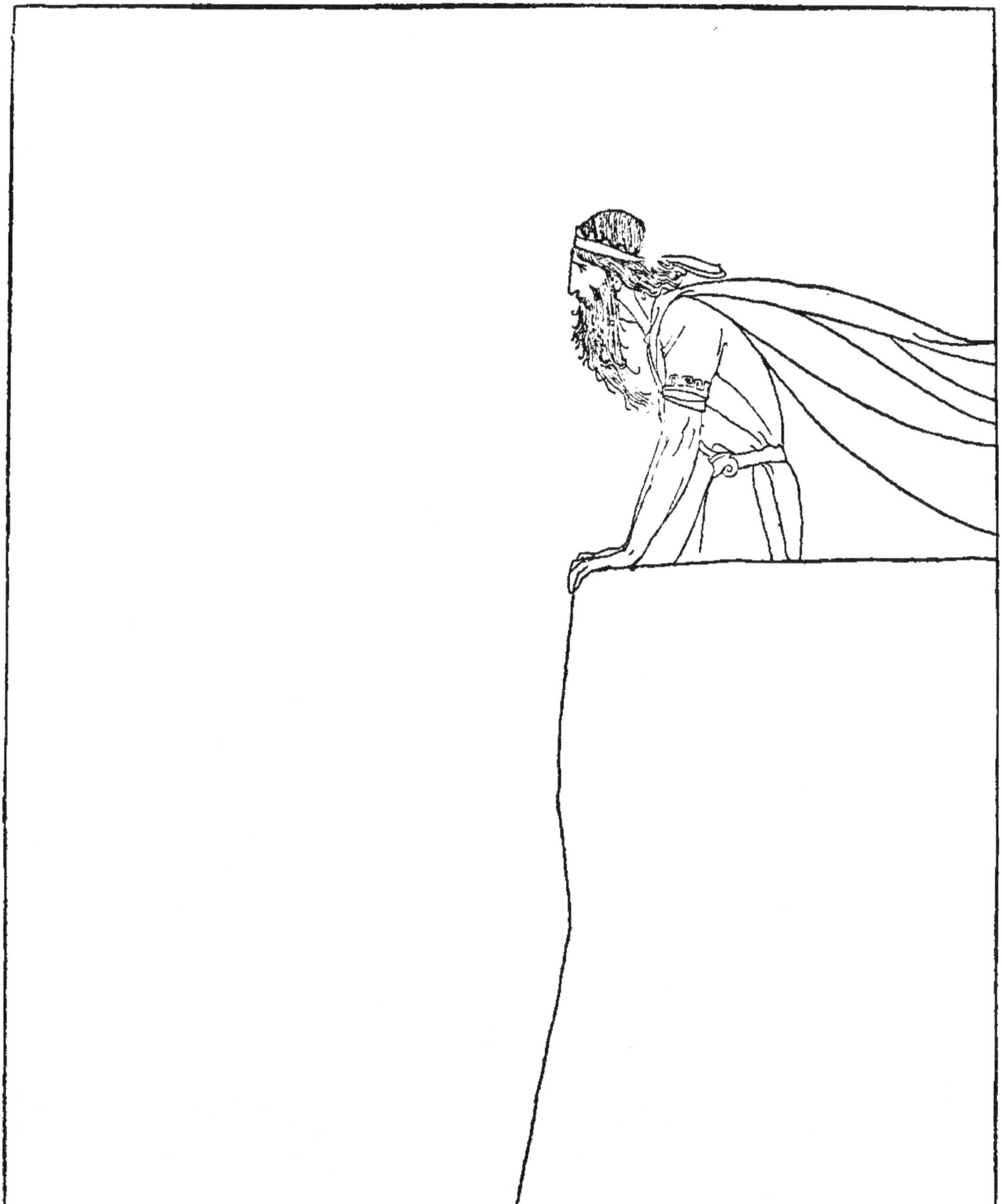

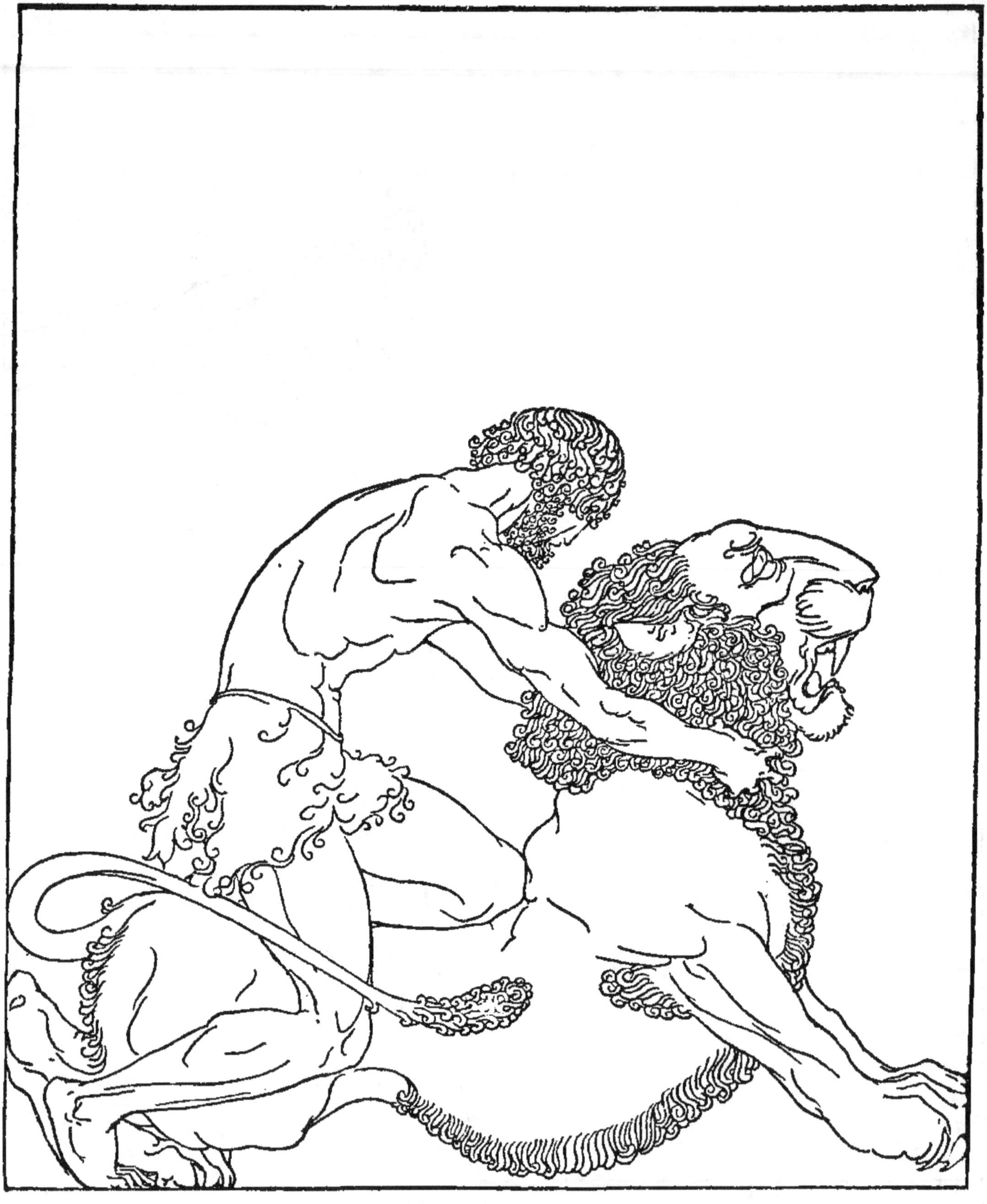

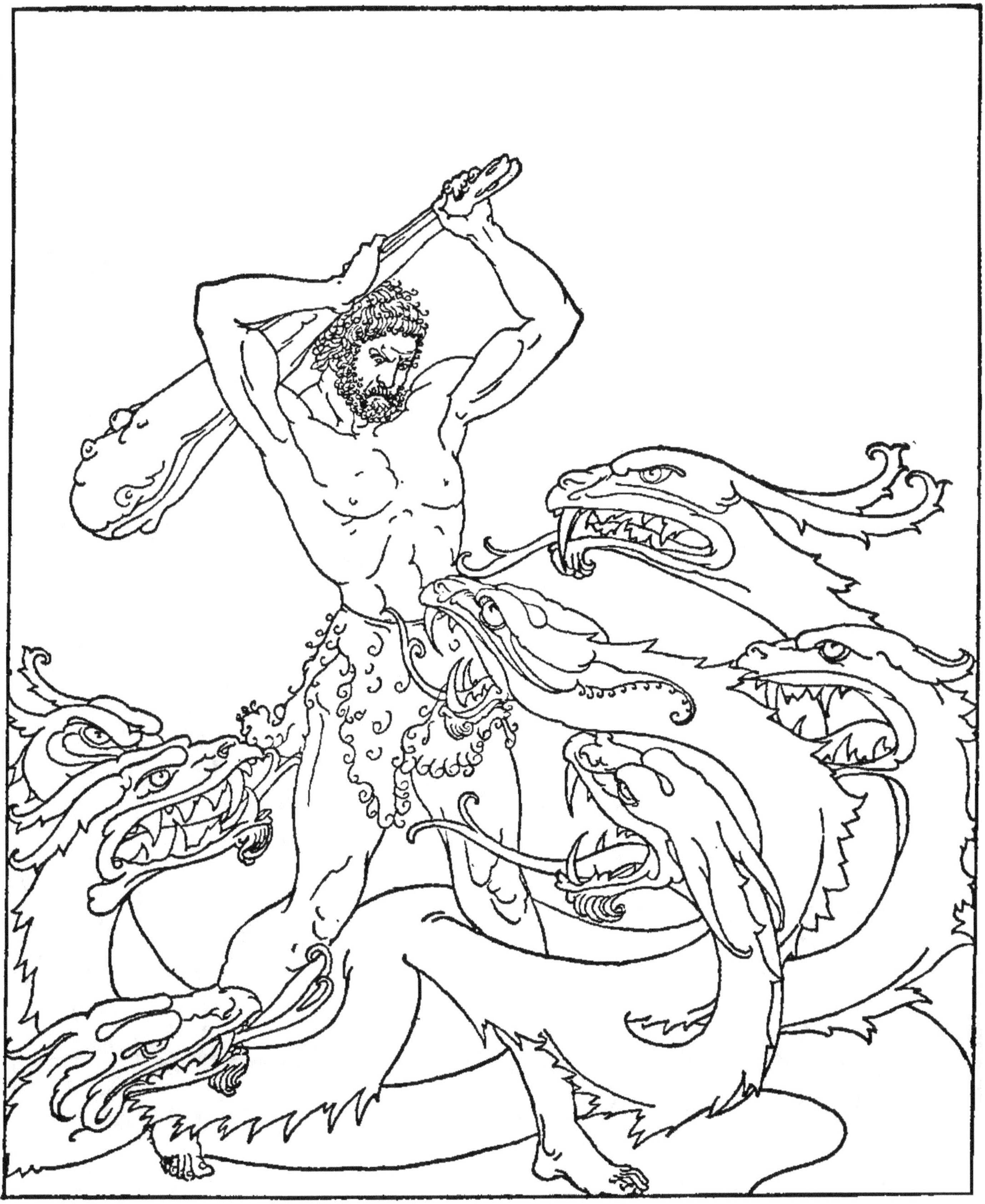

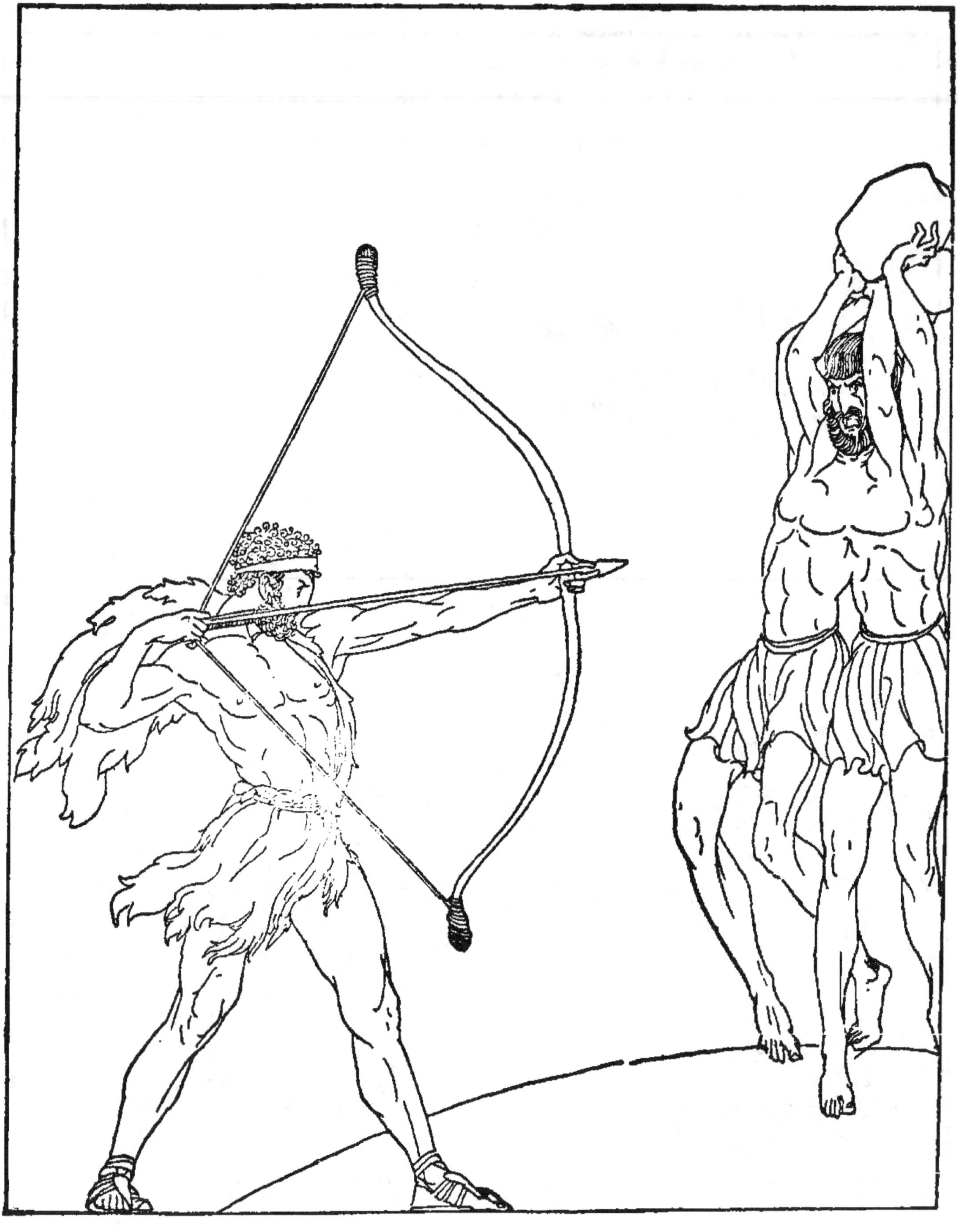

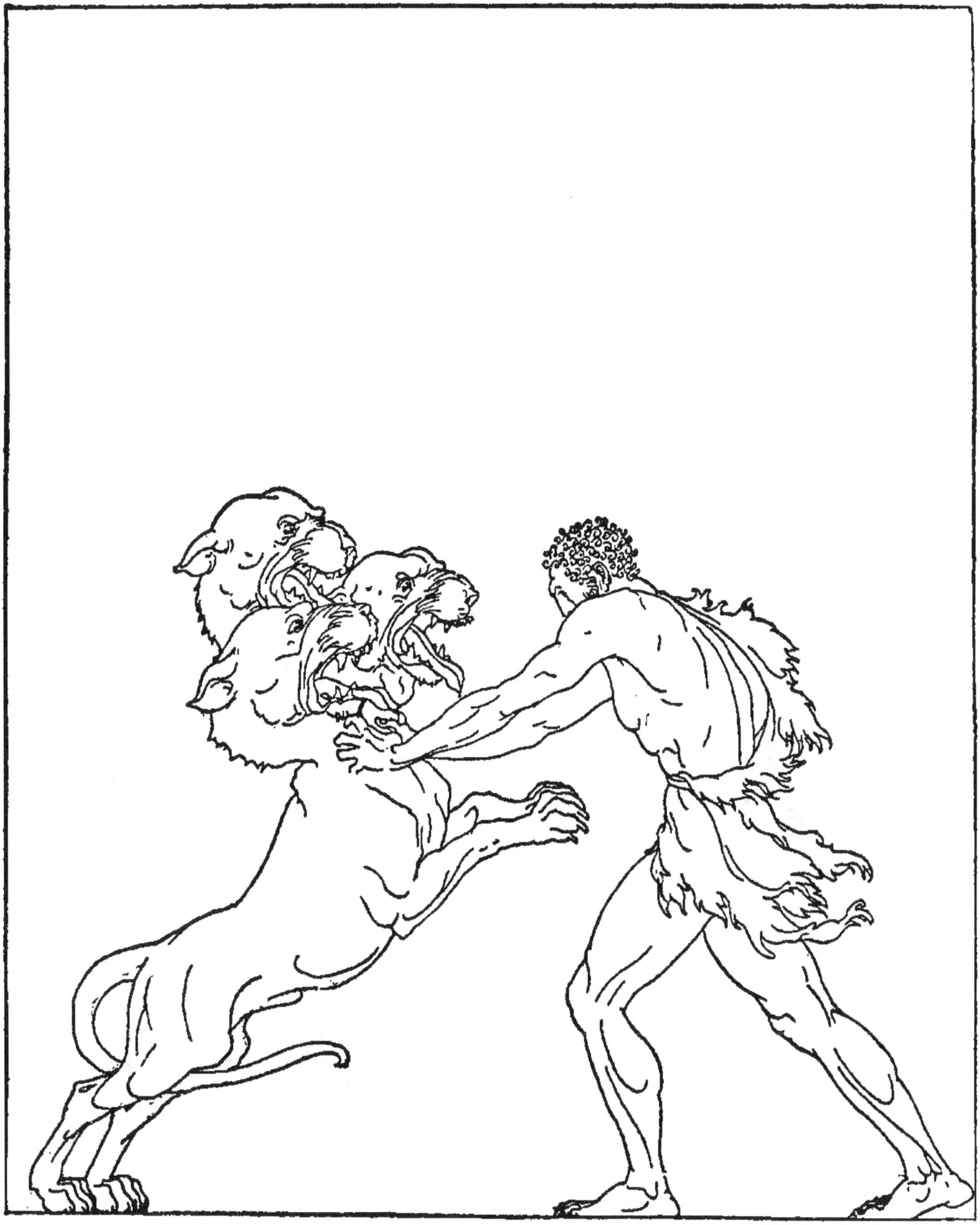

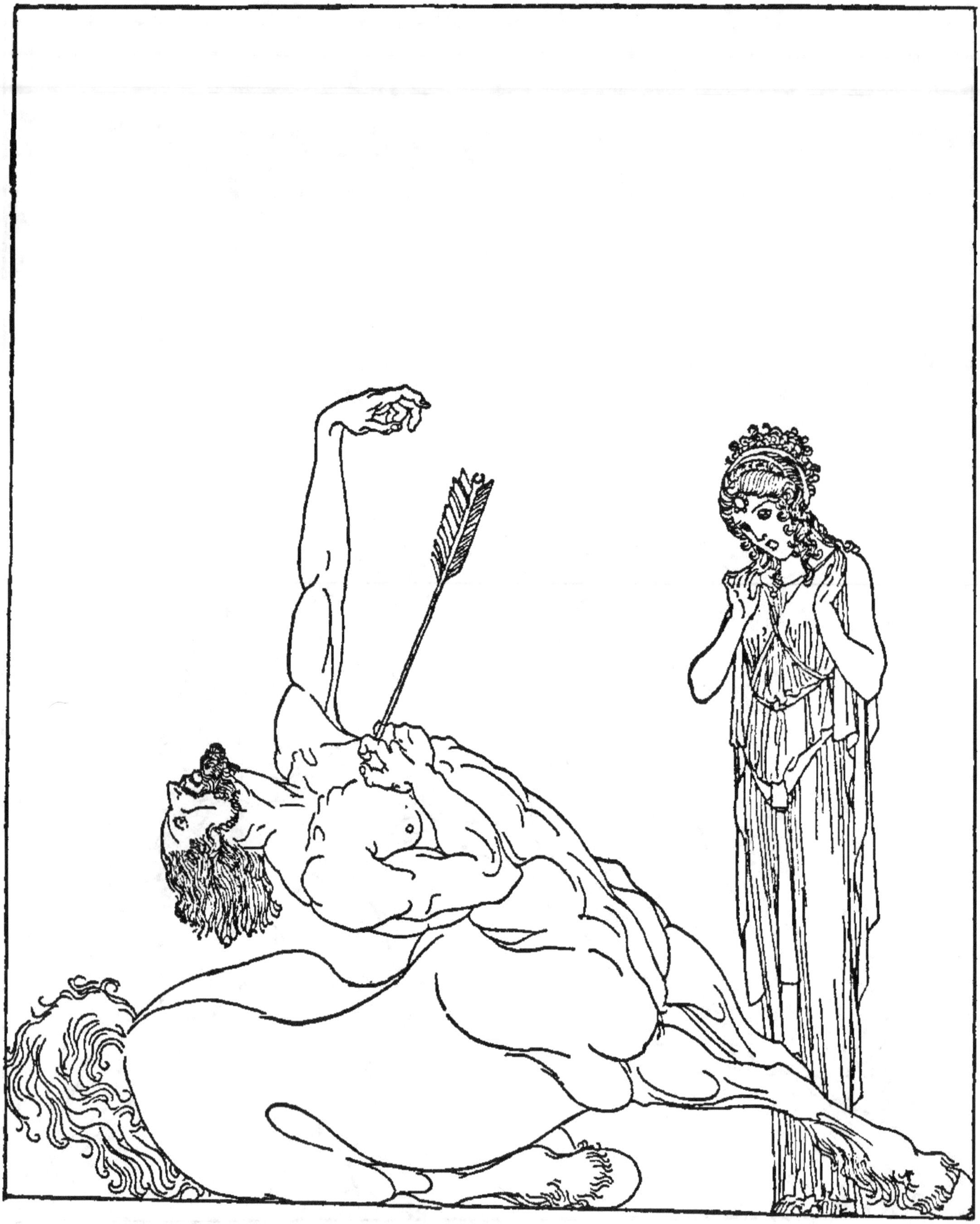

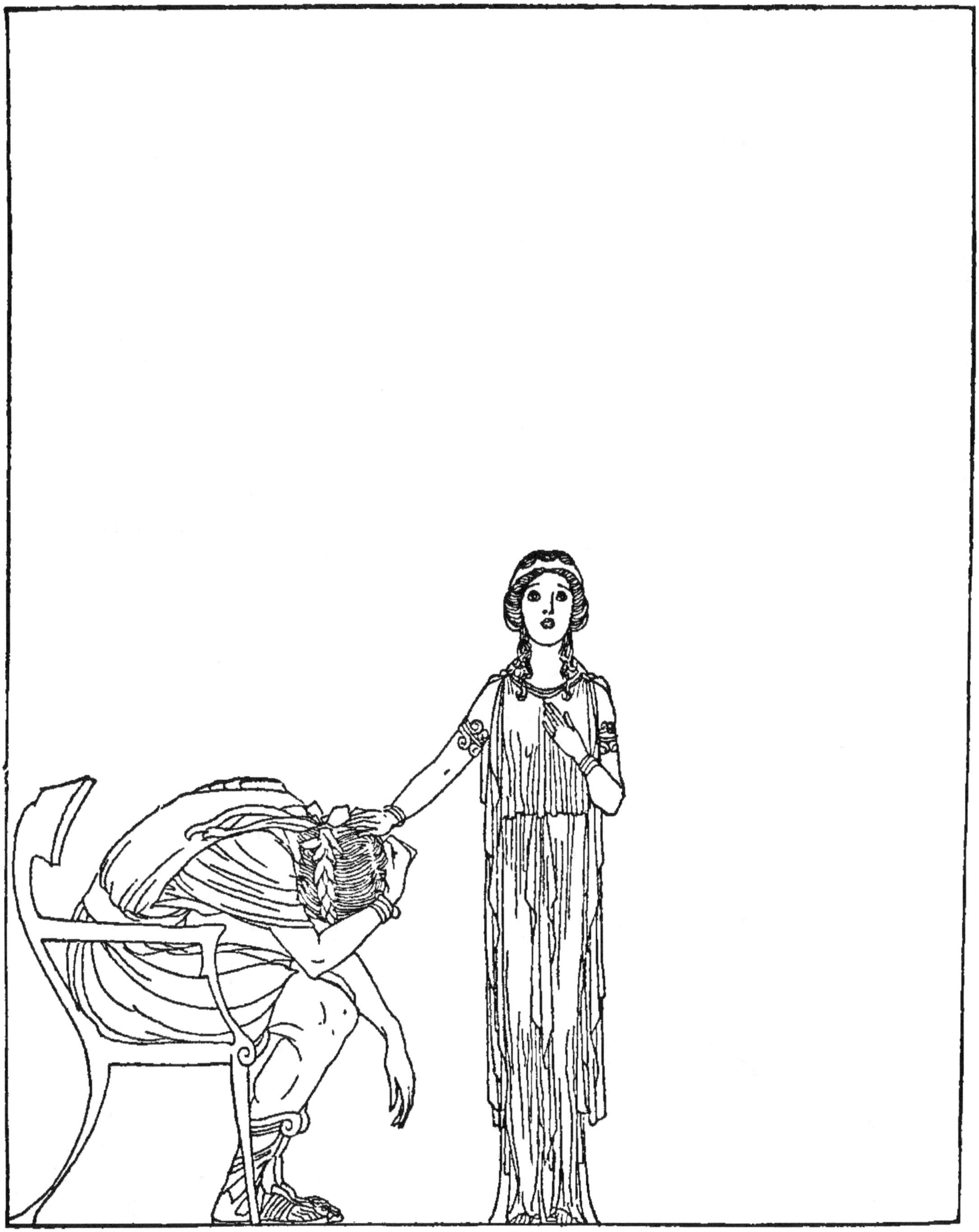

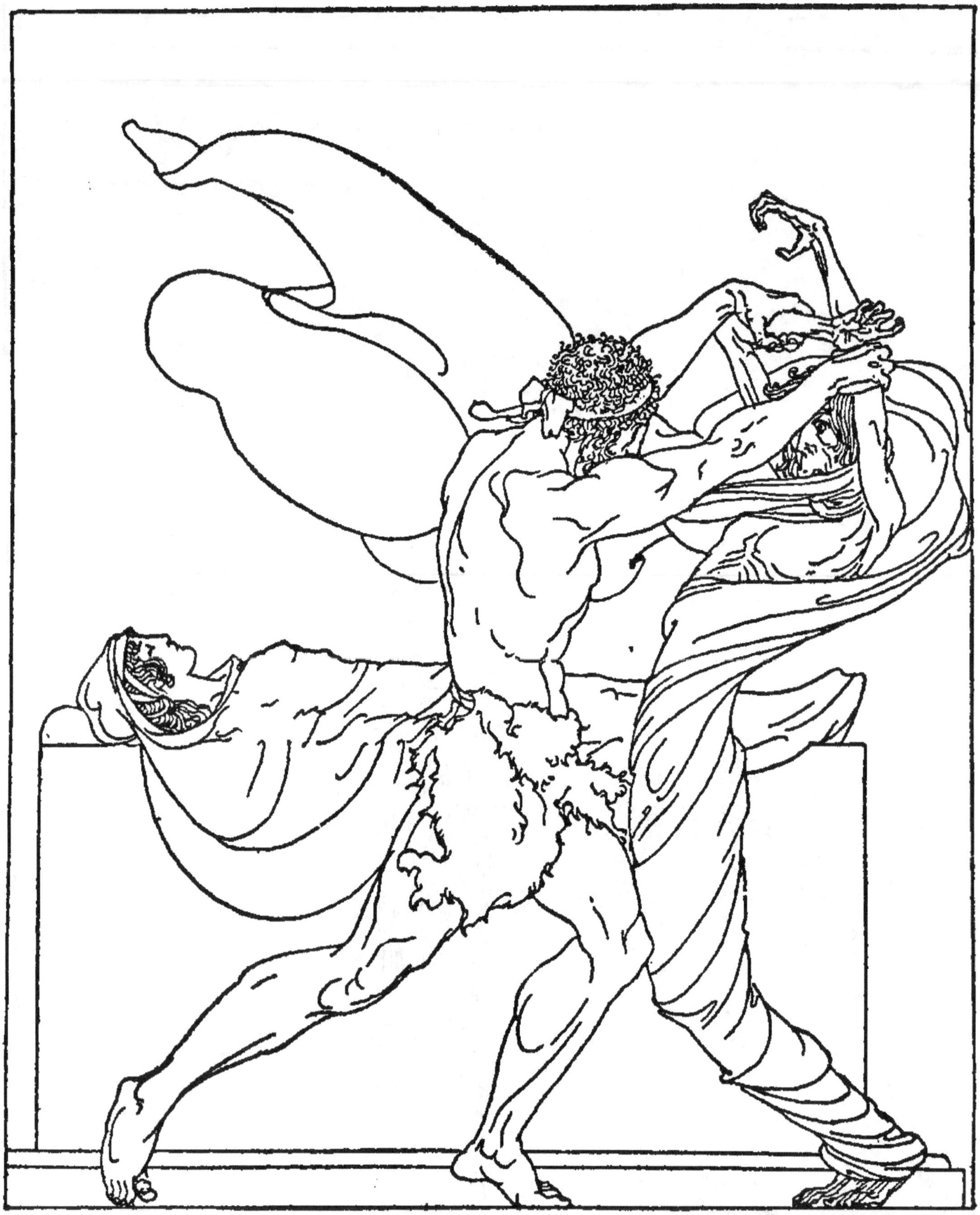

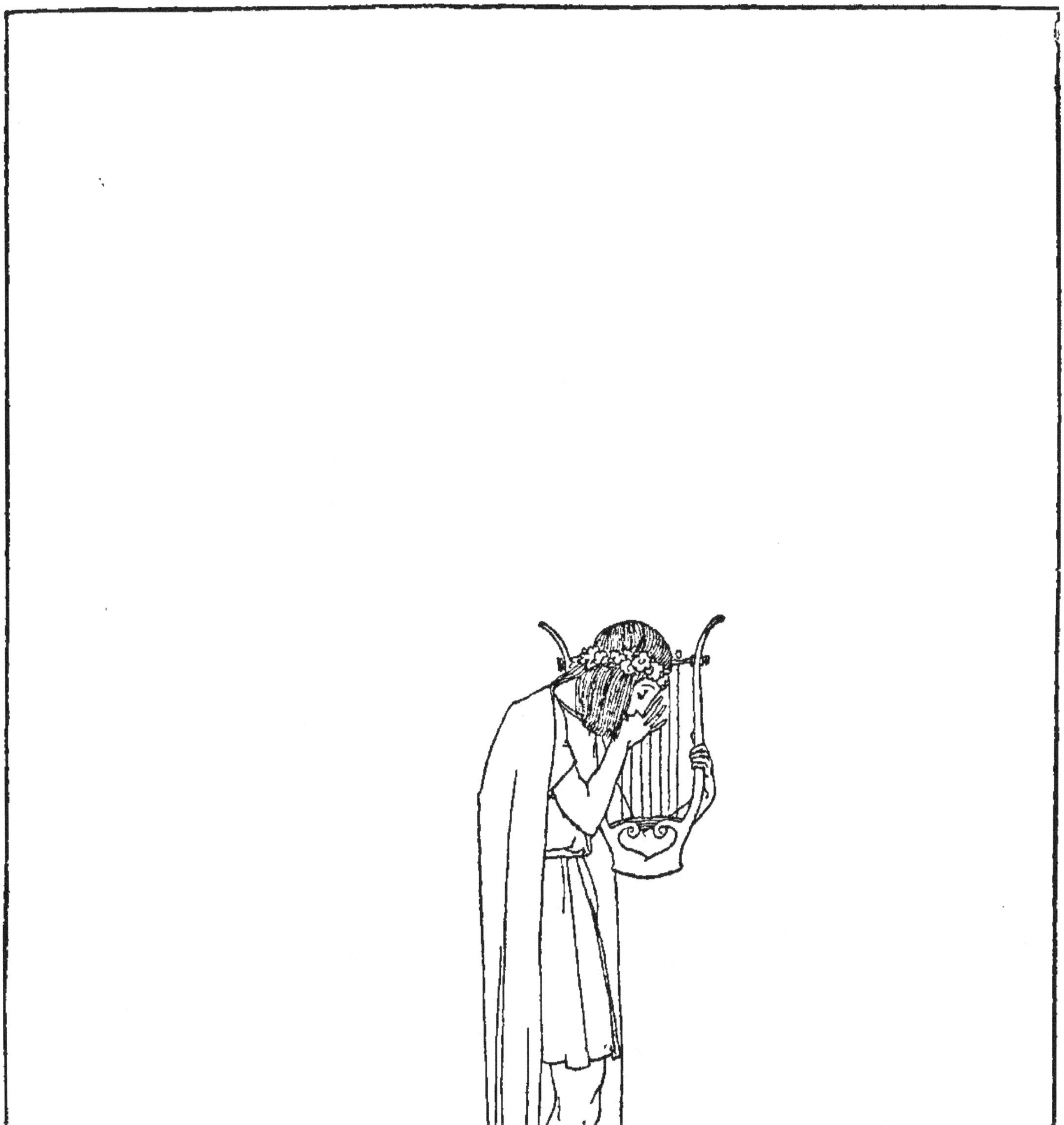

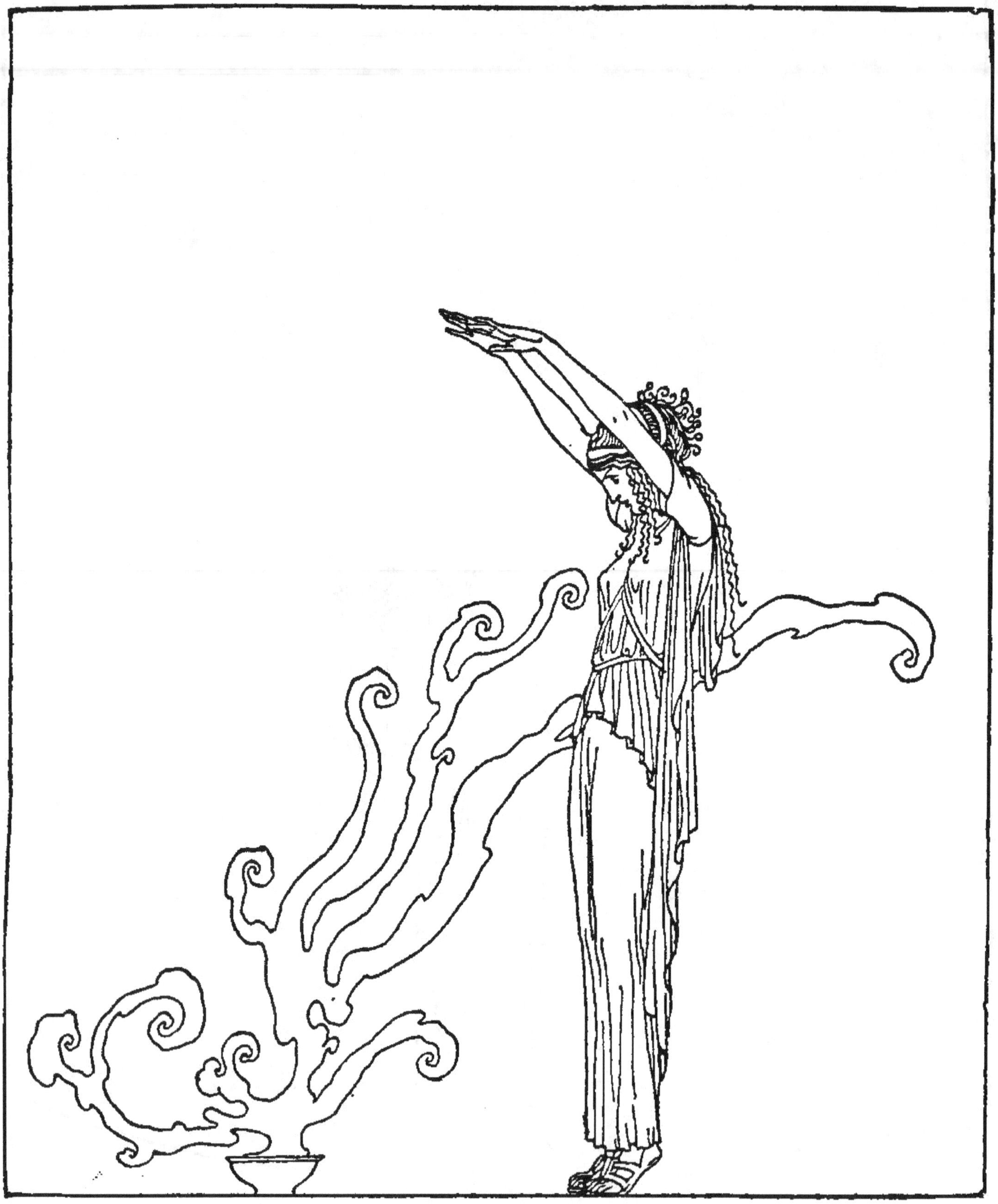

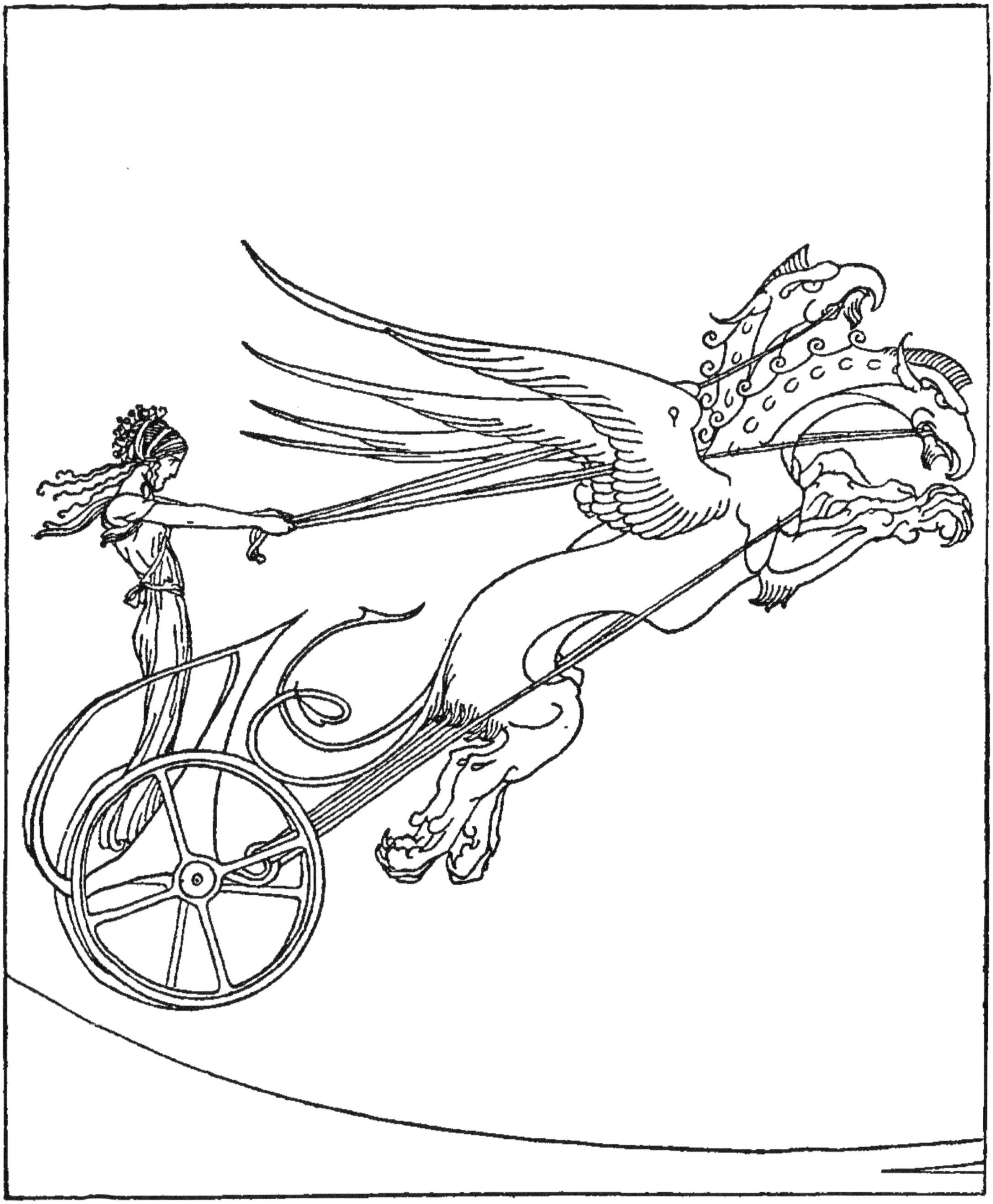